Praise for *Understanding Us & Them*

Understanding Us & Them is a unique approach to understanding oneself and others in order to build relationships with people of all cultures and backgrounds. By using cultural terms, authentic examples, and exercises, readers learn how to increase their Interpersonal Cultural Intelligence (ICQ) and thus create meaningful relationships with the diverse people around them. This is a fresh perspective and a great addition to the resources for building relationships cross-culturally.

> *Patty Lane, Director Intercultural Ministries, Baptist General Convention of Texas, author of* A Beginner's Guide to Crossing Cultures *(IVP)*

This book is funny, and candid, and oh-so-practical; a much-needed resource for groups who want to develop real relationships across lines of difference. Dr. Dykstra-Pruim knows what she's talking about—as a teacher, an academic, a Christian, a mom, a *person* who longs for connection in an increasingly fractured world. These practical lessons offer hard-won wisdom, deep insights, and actual ideas for gaining the skills of interpersonal cultural intelligence. This book is for anyone who wants to connect meaningfully with others, which is a critical, faith-filled calling for each of us. These pages will be bookmarked, underlined, and dog-eared in no time!

> *Rev. Kate Kooyman, Office of Social Justice, Christian Reformed Church in North America*

Weaving theory and practical application seamlessly together, *Understanding Us & Them* offers an engaging resource on Interpersonal Cultural Intelligence for *all* of us. Dr. Pennylyn Dykstra-Pruim speaks with the knowledge and clarity her expertise and lived experience bring, as she guides readers through the ICQ framework with an accessible, encouraging voice. She pairs learning about ICQ with doing ICQ through a variety of exercises designed to foster community and build

relationships. Engaging with others in this small group work takes our understanding of Cultural Intelligence to the next level. By turning ideas into action, Dr. Dykstra-Pruim has given all of us this gift: the tools and opportunity to better understand ourselves and our neighbors.

> *Marla J. Ehlers, Assistant Director, Grand Rapids Public Library and Cultural Intelligence Workshop Facilitator*

I have been waiting for a book like *Understanding Us & Them* for a long time. Dr. Pennylyn Dykstra-Pruim has written a book introducing "Interpersonal Cultural intelligence," a framework born out of years of work as a faculty member and years of lived experience. More than "one more book on cultural intelligence," this book is a "how-to" tool-kit that belongs on the booklist of every person desiring to develop or add content and activities focused on cultural intelligence. Reading this book is like having Dr. Dykstra-Pruim as a personal train-the-trainer coach. This will be my go-to book for years to come.

> *Dr. Michelle Loyd-Paige, Executive Associate to the President for Diversity and Inclusion, Calvin University*

Churches are surprised that their neighborhoods have changed right under their noses with the cultural blessings of the nations. Community meetings are more divided and polarized than ever. Family events have become the frontlines of strife and derision among members. We need help! Pennylyn Dykstra-Pruim has done the research, supplied compelling stories, and provided interactive exercises that cultivate an atmosphere of learning, discovery, and change. My friends, help has arrived for all of us in need of a better way of encountering, embracing, and enjoining ourselves that cultural differences are not only good for us but move us into better spaces of hope.

> *Dr. Reginald Smith, Director of the Offices of Race Relations and Social Justice, Christian Reformed Church in North America*

Understanding Us & Them

Understanding Us & Them

Interpersonal Cultural Intelligence
for Community Building

Pennylyn Dykstra-Pruim

Published 2019 by The Calvin Press
3201 Burton St. SE
Grand Rapids, MI 49546

Publisher's Cataloging-in-Publication Data

Names: Dykstra-Pruim, Pennylyn, author.
Title: Understanding us & them : interpersonal cultural intelligence for community building / Pennylyn Dykstra-Pruim, Ph.D.
Description: Includes bibliographical references. | Grand Rapids, MI: The Calvin Press, 2019.
Identifiers: LCCN 2019943659 | ISBN 978-1-937555-40-5
Subjects: LCSH Intercultural communication. | Cultural relations. | Multiculturalism. | Community organization. | Interpersonal communication. | Interpersonal relations. | Social interaction. | BISAC SELF-HELP / Communication & Social Skills | FAMILY & RELATIONSHIPS / Prejudice
Classification: LCC HM1211 .D95 2019 | DDC 303.48/2--dc23

Cover design: Robert Alderink
Interior design and typeset: TheDesk

All the stories in this book are true and permission has been granted to use them. Some names have been changed to honor the requests of individuals.

Additional resources for *Understanding Us & Them: Interpersonal Cultural Intelligence for Community Building* may be available at www.calvin.edu/press.

Contents

Figures

Introduction

WHY WE NEED THIS BOOK

Thanksgiving with my husband's family in West Michigan is great. Turkey and stuffing, card games and pies. Grandpa always does a short devotional and says a prayer. Grandma always bakes her famous frosted butter horns. We connect with one another, sharing about kids and church and the Black Friday sales. We have a pretty good family dynamic. And we never, ever talk about politics.

Outside my family, I see lots of the opposite: folks argue about political and social issues but often there is no good underlying dynamic between folks of differing opinions. I know I am not the only one who is tired of all the bickering, the eye rolling, the insulting tweets from both sides of the aisle, and the fake news and hateful messaging from different corners on key issues. Sometimes the social media yelling turns into protests or violence, and sometimes into lost lives and souls. We parade our opinions, un-friend persons whose posts annoy us, and don't have many good relationships with people who think very differently from us. I admit my own guilt: I don't have many friends—at least not really good ones—who have significantly different views from mine on the big issues. Some of us step back or look away, feeling that refugees or #blacklivesmatter or #metoo isn't our issue. Unfortunately, mutual ignoring, like much of the current mudslinging, doesn't get us very far.

Welcome to *Understanding Us & Them*. This book is a tool to draw together, to share our stories, and to have conversations that actually help us understand one another. Its design helps groups analyze and explore how culture shapes us. Understanding cultural identities can increase our capacity for getting along, for talking *with* one another and not just *at* one another.

Using this book, we can build Interpersonal Cultural Intelligence (ICQ) and look carefully at what our agendas are. ICQ helps us explore our biases (our hidden agendas), our values and perspectives (our published agendas), and our practices (what we are doing or what we want to do). The agenda for this book is to help individuals and groups build skills and relationships necessary for strong, connected communities. In short, this book is a project in skills building for community building, one attempt to mend some of the divisiveness around us. We don't have to end up agreeing on everything and singing Kumbaya. But we can end up knowing ourselves and the others we engage with in more helpful ways. Mutual understanding and relationship building do not replace the necessary work of fixing policies, changing structures, picking up a hammer literally or figuratively to get some world changing done. But building our ICQ skills will help us to better negotiate our life together.

Some of us work or live in diverse settings. Our neighborhoods or organizations may be more diverse than before. Yet in many places and spaces, minority voices tell us that while diversity may be happening, inclusion lags behind.

Some of us work with organizations that would like to have more diversity, but recruitment and retention efforts haven't gotten the results we want.

Some of us have very little contact with people who are different from us.

Regardless of the amount of diversity in our everyday lives, we all need to develop skills to engage across lines of difference. We may encounter lines of difference at work, on our street, in the news or on social media, or perhaps around our Thanksgiving table. Wherever we encounter people who are different from us and ideas that are different from our own, we can use ICQ to engage with those people and ideas in more helpful ways.

We can't learn to swim if we never go near the water. In the same way, we can't develop ICQ in isolation from others. We need to develop ICQ by learning and engaging with each other. We need one another to learn and practice. What is the bonus when we work on ICQ together?

We get stronger communities. When we learn together in our schools, worshiping communities, workplaces, and neighborhoods, we can grow together.

If you are reading this book in a group, you might be different from or quite similar to others in the group. In either case, reading this book and doing some of the included learning activities together can help you engage with and understand people who are different from you. *Understanding Us & Them: Interpersonal Cultural Intelligence for Community Building* is not a silver bullet for civil discourse or world peace, but it can offer a doable step in the right direction.

Understanding Us & Them opens the door to new connections and strategies for strengthening our communities. In a way, this ICQ project is a bit like piano students learning and practicing scales with the long-term goal of playing their instrument, or like athletes who do sit-ups so they can win a tennis match. The end goal isn't to have a great ICQ but to develop strong communities in which at least some strong connections travel across lines of difference.

HOW TO USE THIS BOOK

In short, you may use this book any way you want, but here is what I recommend. Gather together a group of people who are interested in building community and developing skills for engaging with other people, for understanding other opinions better, for figuring out what is, in fact, the core of their own identities and why. Then work through this book together one chapter at a time. For example, each person reads chapter 1 at home, and then the group gets together to work through some of the included learning and community-building activities for chapter 1.

Each chapter has questions to consider and comes with a learning kit that contains activities to help people talk about and work through the key ideas in that chapter. (All the learning kits are in the second half of the book.) The learning kits provide too many activities for one meeting unless you organize all-nighters. So, one or two people in the group could choose in advance which activities would be best for the group. No one else has to look at the learning kit in advance of the group meeting, but they may if they wish.

It's a fairly simple set-up. Read some on your own and then discuss and learn with others. Since there are five chapters, planning for five group meetings is a good way to start. Give it a try: reach out to neighbors or colleagues or friends. Learn together. Laugh together. Grow community.

BONUS INFORMATION

Almost everyone likes freebies. Check out the notes and resources at the end of each chapter. There you will find additional information or details, related books to read, resources, and film and TV viewing suggestions. Rather than using footnote numbers, comments and citations are keyed to phrases and page numbers.

1

What Is Interpersonal Cultural Intelligence for Community Building?

A QUICK LOOK AT THE CHAPTER

This chapter lays out some cornerstones of Interpersonal Cultural Intelligence (ICQ) for community building, defines some key words, gives reasons why ICQ is critical for us today, and introduces possible learning goals for you and your group through a self-survey.

CORNERSTONE 1: FOCUSING ON CULTURAL IDENTITIES AND BUILDING COMMUNITY

Do you work with, teach, market to, oversee, or serve people who are from a culture or a subculture different from yours? Do you or your organization hope to engage with different groups of people in the best ways possible? Do you want to learn how to understand better the political views on the opposite end of the spectrum from your own? Do you wish you could figure out what the Millennials value most or why Uncle George thinks the things he does? ICQ for community building can help. It is not a cure-all for the puzzling or aggravating differences we encounter, but the skills we build when we learn together with others about ICQ can help us understand not only other people but also other ideas and other ways of seeing the world—even the world of Uncle George.

A quick internet search reveals numerous books, companies, websites, and consultants who offer introductions to Cultural Intelligence, cross-cultural communication, racial reconciliation, and diversity training. Those can be good things to learn for navigating life with others. ICQ for community building is distinguished from those types of training by its first cornerstone: focusing on cultural identities and building community.

This book provides the scaffolding for us to meet and discuss together how to improve our skills for community building and to actually begin building relationships as we learn together about cultures and intercultural skills. Each ICQ for community building group will learn about and improve their ICQ skills as individuals and as a community of learners. We will define and describe ICQ more specifically later in this chapter.

CORNERSTONE 2: LEARNING TOGETHER

I have participated in several one- to three-hour workshops that were great, but then six months or a year later I wondered what difference they made in my life. A second cornerstone of ICQ for community building is that it is designed specifically to allow groups to read and learn together. By exploring ICQ in conversation with others over time (ideally several weeks), we can learn far more about others and ourselves than we can in a short, one-time workshop or by simply reading alone in our own special chair with the cat on our lap. **Learning together is a cornerstone of this project and gives us some firsthand experience reaching out and opening up to others.** We also gain some access to other perspectives, other stories, and other ways of seeing ourselves. And we do all this while getting to know other people.

CORNERSTONE 3: SHARING OUR STORIES

When I visited Cambodia, I met Channery. She was one of our hosts. She cooked for us. She helped organize our interviews with locals. She was one of our cultural insiders—a person who understands Cambodian culture well, has a sense of belonging in that culture, and is recognized by others in that culture as being able to speak for or about that culture in representative ways. Although Channery is an amazing cook, what I appreciated most was her story of life during the Cambodian holocaust under the Khmer Rouge. Suddenly, who she was and wasn't, her love of cooking, the way she raises her children—it all had a specific, personal context. My understanding of Channery *and* of Cambodian history and culture became richer and more textured. She helped me understand how different

> *"Our lives are a collection of stories, truths about who we are, what we believe, what we came from, how we struggle, and how we are strong."*
> —Brené Brown

we are and also how we long for some of the same things. By sharing her stories (and doing so was not easy), she gave me a great gift. As a result, our relationship changed from cordial and kind to personal and unforgettable.

Sharing our stories is a third cornerstone of the ICQ project. **When we tune in to the stories of others, our ideas of them and their world change.** Diversity trainer Patty Digh points out what happens when we share our stories: "You become not a what but a who. Once you are a who, I can't go back to seeing you as a . . . stereotype." Personal stories put a face on that other person or that other group over there. We relate to their human experiences, and they become in our eyes and hearts more human. In addition, stories are compelling. They can help us feel for and understand others in ways that change who we are. As creative writer Reza Aslan has commented, "In order to understand each other, we have to rely on our stories. It's storytelling that builds those relationships. It's stories that change people's minds." So we need to be open to hearing and sharing stories—the short ones of frustrations at the supermarket or school and perhaps also the more difficult ones that offer rich, maybe even painful, glimpses into who we are and why.

KEY WORD: INTERPERSONAL CULTURAL INTELLIGENCE (ICQ)

Interpersonal Cultural Intelligence (ICQ) is the capacity to engage in constructive ways with people who are different from us and with ideas that are different from our own using an understanding of cultures and cultural identities. Building ICQ focuses on three skill areas: (1) knowledge about cultural identities, (2) interpretation of practices and perspectives, and (3) interpersonal skills for interaction and dialogue with others. These three skill areas combine to inform our actions, reactions, and approaches to engaging across lines of difference. (See Figure 1.1.) *Understanding Us & Them* is a book to help groups build their skills for better understanding and interacting with diverse people and ideas while building community through relationships.

Figure 1.1. Interpersonal Cultural Intelligence Graphic

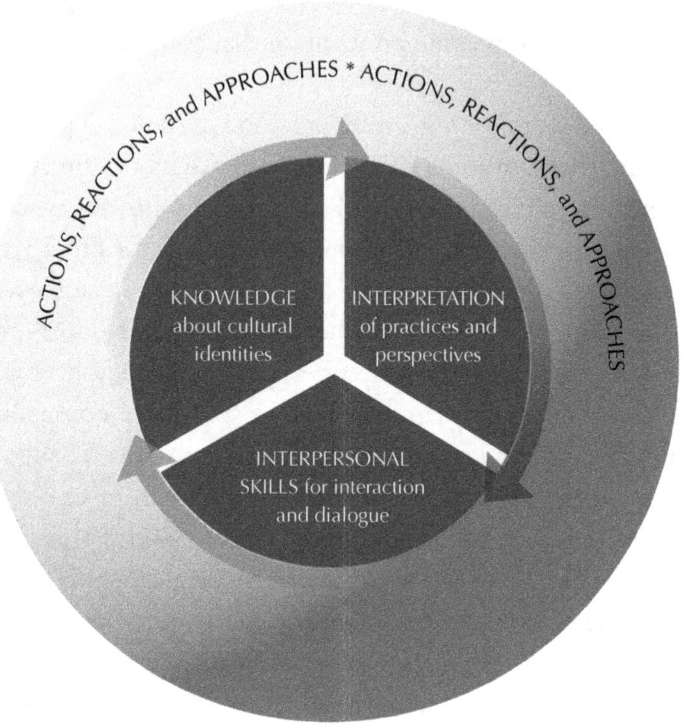

KEY WORD: CULTURE

When we understand more about cultures and how they shape identity, we can better navigate situations in which different cultural backgrounds are playing a role. And, by the way, cultural backgrounds or cultural identities almost always play a role.

We often think about cultures in relation to countries or ethnic groups, such as Chinese culture or Jewish culture. A culture can be defined by other characteristics as well, such as age (Millennial culture, Baby Boomer culture), religion (Southern Baptist culture, Eastern Orthodox culture), physical characteristics (Deaf culture), and common experiences (refugee culture, a particular school culture). Affinity groups, clubs, organizations, and businesses can also have their own culture (a local community-supported agriculture group such as a CSA, the Girl Scouts of America, the National Rifle Association, IBM). For our purposes, **a culture can be a group of persons who are seen** as a group or who identify as a group because they share a common set of rules or expectations for behaviors; similar goals, values, or perspectives; and attachment to or familiarity with many of the same products, practices, and/or experiences.

Of course, the people in a cultural group are not all the same. A culture is a mosaic of differences but with patterns we can observe. The people who identify with a culture have things in common. Sometimes the things they share are choices they have made (vegan culture, *Star Trek* "Trekkie" culture). Sometimes people are born or adopted into a culture (Canadian Mennonite culture, majority US-American culture). My children claim they were born into Green Bay Packer-dom, but that is another story.

Learning about cultural identities is a way of understanding who we are, how we think, and how we act because of the cultures we identify most strongly with. We see our cultural identities in the things we use every day, the behaviors or habits that seem natural to us, and the things we think are important because of the culture or cultures in which we were raised or in which we live or both.

"Every person's mental programming is partly unique, partly shared with others."
—Geert Hofstede

KEY WORD: CULTURAL INTELLIGENCE

I want to mention Cultural Intelligence because it is gaining in popularity, and you may have heard of this already. According to one of the primary spokespersons for Cultural Intelligence, David Livermore, **"Cultural intelligence is a person's capability to function effectively in situations characterized by cultural diversity."** Cultural Intelligence is often called CQ, just as Emotional Intelligence is referred to as EQ. Although CQ has no quotient, as in IQ (Intelligence Quotient), the abbreviation CQ has gained traction, especially in the business and diplomatic worlds. CQ focuses on building concrete skills so that we can be culturally aware and effective, or at least more informed and less clumsy, when we interact across cultural lines.

ICQ differs from Livermore's CQ because of the focus on cultural identities and because of the goal of engaging with different-from-us people and ideas to understand better and to build relationships. CQ focuses on "functioning effectively" in different cultural contexts, which is very important, but ICQ focuses on building community, on exploring and understanding how our cultures shape who we are and how we can understand ourselves and other people and ideas in more helpful ways. **We are using the abbreviation "CQ" to stand for "cultural intelligence" and integrating a focus on the interpersonal. So we're learning about Interpersonal Cultural Intelligence or ICQ for short.**

WHY ICQ?

Why should we use ICQ? Consider this quotation from an article titled "Divided America."

> It's no longer just Republican vs. Democrat, or liberal vs. conservative. It's the 1 percent vs. the 99 percent, rural vs. urban, white men against the world. Climate doubters clash with believers. Bathrooms have become battlefields, borders are battle lines. Sex and race, faith and ethnicity . . . the melting pot seems to be boiling over.

So there is that.

If you have made it this far into chapter 1, you probably understand why ICQ could be a good thing for you, your friends, or your community. However, a few additional notes and quotes can help us convince our neighbor, our supervisor, or Uncle George how valuable ICQ for community building can be.

What the above quotation mentions only indirectly is racism. The long history of racism in the US and its repercussions reflected in the protests surrounding Trayvon Martin, in the debates about incarceration rates of black men, and in the power and media battles over kneeling NFL players will not be solved or healed or put to rest by one book about Interpersonal Cultural Intelligence. But we may be able to better understand the passion and the indifference, the opinions and the beliefs on the different sides of the issues if we work on understanding how cultural backgrounds have shaped our identities and perspectives. That is the work of ICQ. **ICQ for community building can give us tools to use in this important work of talking about and understanding racism and possibly in building more or richer relationships across racial-ethnic lines.**

Need another reason? According to United States Census data and the Pew Research Center, the US population will be majority minority by 2044; in other words, a majority of the population will identify as something other than "majority culture white." Between 2005 and 2050, the US population will increase from 296 million to 438 million. Eighty-two percent of that increase will be from immigrants arriving after 2005 and their US-born children and grandchildren. By 2060, nearly one out of five people will be foreign-born. Estimates show that by 2050, the number of persons self-identifying as more than one race will increase from 2010 numbers by over 226 percent. Similar trends are forecasted in countries such as New Zealand, Germany, and Canada. So at the same time that corporate executives are trying to build their CQ to capitalize on the global economy and international markets, US Americans together with our children and grandchildren will live in communities with people and ideas from diverse cultural backgrounds. If you haven't noticed the opinion wars yet, you will. We can keep to ourselves and create pockets of "us" and "them," or we can nurture twenty-first-century communities that benefit from the diversity that will characterize them.

Mai Chen, who chairs the New Zealand–based Superdiversity Centre of Law, Policy and Business, summarized well what these population changes mean: "It means that employers may soon find that the key skill/capability they are recruiting for is Cultural Intelligence. . . . That ability to work with people from different (and their own unique blended) cultures is going to matter more, whether those people are employees, or customers, or citizens."

The newcomers in our communities and their children, whether they are immigrants from other countries or transplants from the next state over, will also need ICQ as they navigate new cultures or subcultures, biculturality (living in or belonging to two or more cultures), and life in communities marked by blended cultures. The need for ICQ skills among newcomers was eloquently stated by a Somali refugee shortly after arriving in Italy in one of the waves of refugees to Europe in 2015. Asked if he was hoping to travel further to another country, he responded that he wanted to stay in Italy. "I still don't know what freedom means exactly. I have to discover it. I need to learn the language, the laws of the country, its traditions, and how to treat people, how to respect them and how to be respected."

All of us—newcomers as well as the people who are in the dominant culture or feel at home in it—can use ICQ to understand one another better, to build relationships across cultural lines, and to benefit from the diversity that will characterize our twenty-first-century realities. When we learn from one another, integrating the best that our cultures have to offer and practicing how to negotiate differences graciously, we make diversity one of our greatest assets. When we develop skills through ICQ to understand other people and other ideas, we are laying the groundwork for more constructive conversations, for possible compromises, and for hopeful, working relationships. We can grow from loosely affiliated or coexistent ethnic, political, or religious pockets into diverse, multiperspective communities knit together through intentional, personal, and culturally intelligent community building.

If the lines of difference that divide us are not those of country of origin, the lines might be religious, political, or . . . fill in the blank. Even within very stable communities and within the USA itself, some describe the current climate as a "cold civil war." Facebook feeds us the posts it thinks we will "like"; our opinions bounce around in our own echo chambers; in far too many instances, lines of difference have become walls of indifference. This current state of affairs is yet another reason to recommend *Understanding Us & Them* as a next book club read to your circles of friends.

If you are one of the USA's neighbors or allies or even enemies, working with us to figure out why we see the world differently or how we might also share some priorities or perspectives might be worthwhile. We desperately need you as partners in these conversations. We need to learn about and with one another if we are going to make any progress on the problems of our world.

AN ICQ SELF-SURVEY

Let's take a next step in understanding the different skill sets in Interpersonal Cultural Intelligence by taking a self-survey. This survey can help you think about what you already know, what you can learn more about, and your own learning goals. For each statement in the survey, decide how strongly you agree or disagree by circling the appropriate number between 1 (strongly disagree) and 5 (strongly agree). Taking the survey should help you glimpse what you can learn by working through this book, since the survey introduces key parts of the ICQ skill set. After you circle a number for each statement, highlight the items in each section that you are most interested in learning about. Doing so can help you reflect on what you find important in this ICQ learning process.

Figure 1.2. An ICQ Self-Survey

Cultural and Intercultural Knowledge	
I can describe how I am shaped by my cultural upbringing both in general and with specific examples.	1 ②　3　4　5
I can explain how some of the things I do or the way I do things is linked to my ways of seeing the world.	1　2　3　4　⑤
I can explain how things such as fairy tales, foods, and everyday objects are linked to the values and foundational ideas of a culture.	1　2　3　④　5
I know a lot about where my stereotypes of others come from and what sort of stereotypes others might have of me.	1　2　③　4　5
I know a lot about how history and culture affect identity at both a national (political, social) and a personal (emotional, spiritual) level.	1　2　3　④　5
Total out of 25	18

Interpretation of Cultural Practices	
I know a lot about how different cultures think about things such as social hierarchy, individualism, ambiguity, and personal fulfillment.	1　2　3　④　5
I can explain how my personal values influence my actions and reactions in different situations.	1　2　3　④　5
I can explain which of my habits and ideas I am willing to change for the sake of making others feel welcome (or for building consensus in community) and which habits and beliefs are central to my identity.	1　2　3　④　5

I know a lot about ways that my words or actions can be interpreted differently in other cultures.	1 2 ③ 4 5
I know a lot about the religious beliefs and taboos of other cultures and how different cultures express respect differently from how I do.	1 2 ③ 4 5
Total out of 25	18

Interpersonal Skills	
I want to get to know people who are different from me.	1 2 3 ④ 5
I can easily adjust my behaviors based on observations of others' interactions: · verbal behaviors (tone, volume, use of silence, rate of speaking) and · nonverbal behaviors (eye contact, physical proximity, clothing choices, facial expressiveness, hand gestures).	1 2 ③ 4 5
I can be flexible and roll with the punches in new or uncomfortable situations.	1 2 ③ 4 5
I always notice how others are feeling and have good intuitions about why. I am aware of my own emotions, and I monitor and adjust how I interact to compensate when I am in a bad mood.	1 2 3 ④ 5
I am aware of my own biases. I always try to understand the actions and beliefs of others from their perspective.	1 2 3 ④ 5
Total out of 25	18

Time to tally your numbers. For each section, record your score out of 25. Which of the three areas appears to be a strength for you: ICQ Knowledge, ICQ Interpretation, or ICQ Interpersonal Skills? Which statements or areas of learning did you highlight as particularly interesting to you?

In this self-survey you can see some of the concrete things to learn about in each skill area, so taking the survey can help you consider your learning goals while working through *Understanding Us & Them*. For example, the statements under the knowledge section highlight that understanding how our cultures shape us, stereotypes, and identities are important pieces of the puzzle. You can focus on these pieces to gain valuable ICQ knowledge.

You can revisit this survey after working through this book to see how your scores change over time. Perhaps after working through this book, your scores will be different from what they are today. They may be higher or lower. What could that change tell you about yourself?

You can also use this survey as a springboard for discussion. Which statements surprised you? Which were the hardest to choose a number for? If your friends, family, teacher, or supervisor were asked to fill this out for you, how might they score you? What evidence would they have to assign their scores?

THE GAME PLAN

As we conclude chapter 1, let's outline our ICQ-building plan.

- First, learn about cultural identities (how to analyze cultures and what makes us who we are).
- Second, explore and practice how to understand and interpret through cultural lenses (what people do and think, and why).
- Third, consider important factors in interpersonal communication and intercultural dialogue and relations.
- Finally, develop strategies for engaging in more culturally intelligent ways using actions, reactions, and approaches that are smart given what we know about the people and cultures involved.

QUESTIONS TO CONSIDER

1. What did you learn or wonder about as you were doing the self-survey?
2. What got you interested in participating in an ICQ for community building book group?

NOTES AND RESOURCES

Quotations in this chapter are taken from Brené Brown, *The Hustle for Worthiness.* DVD. United States: 3C Press. 2010; Geert Hofstede, *Culture's Consequences: International Differences in Work-Related Values* (Thousand Oaks, CA: SAGE Publications, 2003), 2.

7 **even the world of Uncle George:** Although not a focus of this book project, Interpersonal Cultural Intelligence can also help families and communities bridge generational divides. In general, generations share a set of historical events, national experiences, and a consciousness of social movements that form part of their collective memory and shape their identities. The US Census and Pew Research data also indicate that as the Baby Boomers age into retirement, the "older" generation will be a larger percentage of the whole than it is today. See "Census Summary 2014-2060" cited below. A glimpse into how ICQ can help us think about differences cross-generationally is offered in chapter 3: the nylons example.

9 **Patty Digh:** See her TED Talk "Grant Specificity to the Other," accessed June 27, 2018, https://www.youtube.com/watch?v=3hVReRJCTHU.

9 **Reza Aslan:** See his TED Talk "Unity in Diversity," accessed June 27, 2018, https://www.youtube.com/watch?v=VgLAzwgizdk.

9 **be open to hearing and sharing stories:** If your book group is pretty homogenous, you may want to seek out cultural insiders from other backgrounds to partner with your group. Good films or stories that the cultural insiders feel represent their culture can also be good resources.

11 **Cultural Intelligence:** The Cultural Intelligence framework originated with the theoretical work of P. Christopher Earley and Soon Ang, *Cultural Intelligence: Individual Interactions across Cultures* (Stanford, CA: Stanford University Press, 2003). Over the past decade, different persons have worked with the CQ framework, and different publications sometimes use different cover terms for the different CQ skill areas. For example, David Livermore, in his more recent publications, uses "drive" to talk about motivations, specifically our motivation to engage with others and persevere through challenging situations. Regardless of how the skills are grouped or exactly defined, the basic CQ frameworks are similar in their focus on concrete skill building and the skill areas involving knowledge, interpretation, behaviors, and motivations. A short introductory video can be found at https://www.youtube.com/watch?v=SMi7yhHjASQ, accessed February 7, 2019.

11 **David Livermore:** A very accessible introduction to cultural intelligence can be found in the books by David Livermore. He has written books for different audiences, including those involved in short-term missions and business professionals, for example. See *Serving with Eyes Wide Open* (Grand Rapids, MI: Baker Books, 2006); and *The Cultural Intelligence Difference: Master the One Skill You Can't Do Without in Today's Global Economy* (Nashville, TN: AMACOM, 2011). The Cultural Intelligence Center, directed by Livermore, targets businesses and organizations interested in consultant services for CQ assessment and training. See https://culturalq.com/.

12 **ICQ differs from Livermore's CQ:** Regarding *CQ strategy:* In recent iterations of the CQ framework, "strategy" is used as a cover term for learning how

to interpret what is going on in a cross-cultural situation as well as how to plan to avoid misunderstandings as needed. This use of "strategy" is thus quite similar to our use of "interpretation," which was the term used in some early versions of the CQ model. Livermore's idea of strategy also includes an ability to be flexible with our actions and plans as needed. This flexibility is inherent throughout the different skill areas as we focus on being more open-minded and open-hearted to people who are different from us and to cultures and ideas that are different from our own. The skill of flexibility is also highlighted in our work in chapters 3 and 4.

Regarding *CQ drive:* In CQ models, the term "drive" refers to our motivations for engaging cross-culturally. This is critical to success. For our goals of working mostly at a personal level on relationships across cultural lines, understanding the motivations of ourselves and those we are engaged with is, of course, important. I have linked this broader focus on motivations to interpretation so that we focus on why we do what we do and why we think how we think. Much of what motivates us in life is linked to our cultural upbringings and biases. This is admittedly a slightly different focus on motivations, but it is crucial in our work to understand ourselves and others better. Livermore's additional use of drive to mean our perseverance through difficult situations is addressed when we look in chapter 5 at our approach to this entire ICQ for community building project.

12 **"It's no longer just Republican vs. Democrat":** "Divided America," Associated Press, accessed June 13, 2018, https://www.ap.org/explore/divided-america/.

13 **important work of talking about and understanding racism:** The work of Joy DeGruy Leary may interest persons looking to understand how the history and experiences of forced migration and slavery have shaped segments of African American culture today. See Joy DeGruy Leary, *Post Traumatic Slave Syndrome: America's Legacy of Enduring Injury and Healing* (Milwaukie, OR: Uptone Press, 2005).

13 **United States Census data and the Pew Research Center:** These summaries are taken from the following reports, all accessed June 12, 2015: "Census Summary 2014–2060," https://www.census.gov/newsroom/press-releases/2015/cb15-tps16.html; "Census Report 2014–2060," http://www.census.gov/content/dam/Census/library/publications/2015/demo/p25-1143.pdf; and "Pew Data 2005–2050," http://www.pewhispanic.org/2008/02/11/us-population-projections-2005-2050/, accessed February 7, 2019.

13 **Mai Chen:** She won a New Zealand Law Foundation Grant to research superdiversity, especially its impact on electoral law and policy. Her quotations in this book are from her editorial "NZ Melting Pot Needs Special Cooks," *New Zealand Herald,* June 4, 2015, A29.

13 **Superdiversity:** Steven Vertovec defined this in his article "New Complexities of Cohension [sic] in Britain: Super-Diversity, Transnationalism, and Civil-Integration,"

2007, accessed June 12, 2015, https://www.compas.ox.ac.uk/2007/er-2007 -complexities_cohesion_britain_cic/. "*Super-diversity* is a term intended to underline a level and kind of complexity surpassing anything the country has previously experienced. 'Super-diversity' is distinguished by a dynamic interplay of variables, including: country of origin (comprising a variety of possible subset traits such as ethnicity, language[s], religious tradition, regional and local identities, cultural values and practices), migration channel . . ., and legal status."

14 **Somali refugee:** This quotation is from an interview conducted in June 2015 by a reporter from Al Jazeera. "Migrants Tell Their Stories after Rescue on Lampedusa," YouTube, accessed from New Zealand June 12, 2015, https://www.youtube .com/watch?v=tUtlpwsRZYE.

14 **cold civil war:** Livia Gershon, "Just How Divided Are Americans Since Trump's Election," History, November 8, 2017, https://www.history.com/news/just-how -divided-are-americans-since-trumps-election, accessed April 25, 2019.

16 **Interpersonal Skills:** Such skills are recognized as critical in our intercultural interactions. In certifying trainers and assessing individuals, the Intercultural Development Inventory (IDI, LLC) includes self-assessments of one's intercultural conflict style in addition to the standard intercultural development assessment. Conflict styles and an awareness of our own communication preferences can prove important in all our personal interactions, including those across cultural lines. See https://idiinventory.com/.

Film Suggestions

Outsourced (2006) PG-13. An American midlevel sales executive is sent to India to train a local to do the job after his entire department is outsourced to that country. Cultural misunderstandings and intercultural insights are woven into this romantic comedy.

The Joy Luck Club (1993) R. The stories of four Asian American daughters and their mothers are woven together in a compelling drama. The connections and disjunctions highlight how different cultural backgrounds and personal stories form our identities. This is rated R for mature content.

2

I and We—
ICQ Knowledge

A QUICK LOOK AT THE CHAPTER

This chapter looks at ICQ knowledge by exploring what culture is and how it shapes or affects us, how powerful bias is, and how we can understand the building blocks of culture—products, practices, and perspectives—by using the Three P's Tool.

KEY WORD: ICQ KNOWLEDGE

ICQ knowledge is knowing about our own cultural identities and about how cultures differ. This knowledge includes realizing how powerful stereotypes are. Over the next few chapters, we will become familiar with some ways of analyzing and thinking about cultures and cultural identities. We will improve our ability to analyze and explain the meaning of products, practices, and perspectives from inside their cultural contexts. We will focus on some knowledge useful to describe or understand a culture and cultural identities.

CULTURAL IDENTITIES ARE COMPLICATED

How do you introduce yourself? If I am asked to introduce myself in a casual group setting, I might say something like this:

Hi, I'm Penny. I'm from Grand Rapids, Michigan. I'm a professor. I have three kids. And I enjoy cooking, knitting, and hiking, but *not* up steep hills for more than ten minutes at a time.

But what if I introduced myself like this instead:

Greetings to you all! My canoe is Tinana. My mountain is Whangatauatia. My river is Karirikura te Moana. My people group is Te Rarawa. My community leader is Ko Poroa. My place to stand and belong is Roma. My name is Haami Piripi. Greetings! Greetings! Greetings!

If this were my personal introduction, I would be a completely different person, not only because of what I said but also because of how I said it, what parts of my identity I emphasized, and which facts about who I am I chose to share in a casual introduction.

As you may have guessed, the second introduction is from a culture that values ancestral ties to places and people. The greetings at the beginning and end are important because they formally recognize the group, even though this is a relatively informal introduction. In this culture, the connection to a chief is important, just like the connection to the water and the mountains close to home. This personal introduction is representative of a type of introduction called a *mihi* in the Maori culture. (Maori refers to the native peoples of Aotearoa, commonly known as New Zealand.) A *mihi* is usually given in the Maori language and is learned by many schoolchildren in New Zealand. In the Maori culture, a person's social-political leader, mountains or bodies of water near their home, and their hometown come together to form their *Whakapapa*—their lineage or "layers of me."

So what could my particular Midwestern, US-American introduction tell us about my home culture or about my subculture, a cultural group within a larger culture? Let's take a closer look.

Figure 2.1. Analysis of Penny's Introduction of Herself

Hi	This is a pretty casual greeting. If I started with, "Ladies and gentlemen, it is a privilege to introduce myself to you," *that* would be really weird.
I'm Penny	The use of my first name and only my first name seems friendly. That is the most important part of my name anyway, because that is what others will probably call me later. In some cultures, the family name is so much more important that it comes first and the individual name comes afterward. In my cultures, if someone introduces herself with, "Hello, I am Dr. Jones," that might sound a little snobby, first because she felt she needed to use a title (as if she might be better than others) and second because she did not include her first name (so that no one can feel as if they are on a first-name basis with her). Certain medical doctors in hospitals say, "I'm Dr. So-and-So" so that patients know they are the doctor and because they do not intend to get too friendly, since they are establishing a professional doctor-patient relationship.

Grand Rapids	Is this where I live now or where I was born or where my grandfather was raised? You do not know from what I said. But if you also have a connection to West Michigan, then you might talk to me later, and we can start a conversation about Grand Rapids. We might even play some sort of who-do-you-know Bingo game.
professor	A job or profession is often one of the first facts that we share in my cultures. If we do not volunteer this information, we usually get asked, "So, Bob, what do you do (for a living)?" We give out this information easily. We do not bother to mention the river nearest our house or the name of our town mayor.
three kids	In professional interviews in the US, inquiring about personal relationships or family status is generally illegal. In other cultures, talking about how much a person needs a job because they are caring for parents or have children to support would be acceptable. In a casual introduction in my cultures, we usually include something about our families. If people avoid talking about their families, we might think there are issues or dysfunctions.
hobbies	In my cultures, hobbies make us seem like humans with weekends. Our jobs are important, but so is the fact that we do things other than work, even if those things aren't very interesting.
humor	In my small cultural bubble, humor tinged with humility is a positive, though sarcasm is not. Almost any presentation, sermon, lecture, or casual introduction can include a joke or a humorous comment to put people at ease. The safest person to make a joke about is oneself, otherwise we might get in trouble for being politically incorrect or . . . boring.

You may be thinking, *Well, that was a long closer look.* Yes, something as simple as a five-sentence introduction of yourself is actually culturally complex! Also, we may say different things about ourselves depending on if we are in a university class or a Weight Watchers meeting or a cancer support group. How we describe ourselves to others depends on our cultural contexts—the big cultures (such as US–American or Midwestern US–American) and the smaller cultures (such as a birthing class, an Alcoholics Anonymous group, or the First Baptist Church). All the cultures we are part of have expectations of what we say (content) and how (formality, style) we introduce ourselves. We know or, rather, automatically follow these expectations if we are natives or very familiar with and comfortable in those cultures and if we have a usual amount of Social and Emotional Intelligence. **Our cultures have taught us**

appropriate or acceptable behaviors and ways of talking in specific situations.

One could argue that our cultures have programmed us to act and react in certain ways. We humans are born with some basic programming or an "operating system," if you will. We or our brains are wired to learn a language and to categorize what we encounter (people, plants, animals, objects) as familiar or new, as insider or outsider. The cultures in which we are raised and live take us humans with our operating systems and provide the "mental programming," helping us to survive by giving us information to categorize things in life as safe or dangerous. (See Figure 2.2.)

Figure 2.2. We Are Shaped by Our Cultures

Some of our traits or ways of doing things are hardwired, and some are learned. Nonetheless, **the cultures in which we are raised and in which we live have a huge impact on how we see the world,** what we think of as normal or logical or even right. Of course, we are individuals, not robots produced in a culture factory. What we think and do and say are determined by many things, including the fact that we are human beings with different experiences and personalities. **Our unique individual personalities and experiences also affect who we are; how we react, act, and interact; and how we understand the world.**

"Most of us tend to underestimate the degree to which we ourselves are a product of culture. It is much easier to see it in others."
—David Livermore

How we introduce ourselves and the types of things that seem normal to talk about when we do so are examples of how we are products of a culture. We have expectations of how people act and what people should say in certain contexts because we have a specific culture that affects how we filter and experience our world. If we had grown up in a different culture, we might well have different expectations. **We see things as right or normal or logical against the backdrop of our specific cultures. In other words, key pieces of our identities—what makes us how we are—are also shaped a great deal by our cultures.**

KEY WORD: STEREOTYPES

Stereotypes are the simplified ideas we have and the mental or actual labels we put on things and people based on limited or selected information.

Stereotypes could be renamed "mono-types" because they are based on limited information and arise as our brains try to be efficient in categorizing things as in or out, safe or dangerous. Monotyping says, "I'm seeing that group over there as one sort of thing." This is what we do to outsiders. Sociologist Christena Cleveland says we see outsiders as all similar to each other in the things that matter most. In contrast, we see insiders as unique and thus interesting.

> "It is never too late to give up our prejudices."
> —Henry David Thoreau

MULTIPLE PERSPECTIVES ON TARANTULAS

Hairy tarantulas used to be, in my opinion, just scary-looking bugs in science books until my third-grade daughter came home and told me that her class pet was (you guessed it) a tarantula. "She's really sweet!" my daughter gushed. "Her name is Charlotte." Of course, Charlotte was not just a hairy, eight-legged creepy-crawly. Charlotte was an amazing curiosity. I learned through my daughter that there are hundreds of kinds of tarantulas, some as big as a dinner plate! Charlotte was just the right size to fit in your hands, so everyone wanted to hold her. Female tarantulas can live thirty or forty years. Charlotte was about twenty years old, so if we took care of her, she could live until the entire class graduated from high school. I was still not convinced to volunteer for spider duty over Christmas break. Fortunately, I did not have to step up, because one day Charlotte mysteriously went missing (and for the record, I had nothing to do with that).

Years later, when I saw Peter Jackson's *Lord of the Rings* movies, I was predictably horrified by those convincing, gigantic, hobbit-eating tarantulas. It is a good thing that my daughter was well beyond third grade by then. She was able to discern that those monsters on the screen were from Tolkien's imagination. All Jackson had to do was add my early ideas of "scary-looking bugs," blow them up literally bigger than life, mix them with spooky music and dark tunnels, and voilà! He had spine-tingling movie scenes that made my skin crawl.

Fast-forward to my first trip to Cambodia. My friends informed me that in certain places you can buy fried tarantulas. If you are curious, here is how they are made. After you catch and defang them, you wash them and then toss them in a combination of sugar and dried chicken soup mix. Then you fry them in oil for about three minutes or until most of the hair is off. Yum, right? I figured that I might actually have to work up the courage to give fried tarantulas a try, as a good example for the group of students I was leading on the trip. At that moment, neither the memory of sweet Charlotte nor those nasty spider-beasts from Tolkien's Middle Earth were much use. What did help was researching how the tarantulas were caught and prepared, listening to others who had already tasted tarantula, and convincing myself that even though eating spiders was not part of my American dream, I could do it for the sake of the experience and the message it might send to my students.

My early associations with tarantulas are not surprising, given my home culture. I was not alone in thinking large spiders are ugly and scary and not appetizing. Some people are so afraid of spiders that it becomes an irrational fear. I *know* that those computer-generated monstrous spiders are not real. Thankfully, there are no five-foot-tall spiders in real life! But when I see large tarantulas in zoos or even large unrelated bugs in the woods, I still have to fight my "yuck" reaction. After all, my shivers when I watch the character Frodo get stung by the spider-monster *are* real, and that experience adds to all my negative stereotypes of spiders, making it even harder for me to order, pay for, and eat tarantulas in Cambodia.

The scary images and ideas in my head also affect my reaction to the idea of my daughter snuggling Charlotte. And my daughter's experience with Charlotte makes her appalled that I would think about eating a tarantula. Add another perspective: the Cambodian vendor who makes her living cooking and selling tarantulas may capitalize on the "gross factor" of her goods among the tourists, but she is counting on making her sales to put rice on the plates of her children.

All these stories and more are needed to begin to understand the stereotypes of "tarantulas." Any one perspective can have validity, but it is also biased and missing pieces of the whole picture. The writer Chimamanda Ngozi Adichie captured a great insight about stereotypes: "The single story creates stereotypes. . . . The problem with stereotypes is not that they are untrue, but that they are incomplete. They make one story become the only story."

None of my associations or reactions or experiences alone reflect the entire truth about tarantulas, and, of course, the big-screen and big-in-our-imagination ideas about hairy, eight-legged, blood-sucking monsters are pretty inaccurate from any real-world point of view. We *know* this, but those movie images still affect how we think, feel, and react. **So even as we are learning about how powerful and pervasive stereotypes can be, we might still react emotionally or physically based on stereotypes. The important step forward is to recognize such reactions for what they are.**

STEREOTYPES BLIND US

Imagine we carry a pad of sticky notes in our back pockets that represents the vast collection of stereotypes in our minds. When we meet people or read about them, we consciously or unconsciously place sticky notes (stereotypes) onto them. The associations or clichés in our minds can effectively cover up the faces of others we meet. **Sometimes we have so many preconceived notions (some we are aware of and many we don't realize are there) that we are disabled from seeing who others truly are.**

Figure 2.3. Stereotypes Blind Us from Seeing Others

Diversity trainer and communication specialist Steve Robbins, among others, outlines how our brains are wired to use "typing" to help us efficiently make sense of the world around us. Robbins uses research from neuroscience to explain how our brains are wired to quickly identify insiders and outsiders. Often, we do this with very little information. Once we categorize someone or something as an outsider, moving him, her, or it to the safe or insider group in our minds can take a long time and lots of counter information.

If the last gray dog we encountered tried to bite us, we might shy away from the next gray dog. If we have been chased and bitten by more than one gray dog or if we watched a movie recently about a mean gray dog, we can be very quick to avoid the mottled canine we spy in our neighborhood. We might "type" all gray dogs as dangerous, ignoring all the information we could observe to make a more informed judgment, such as the pitch and intensity of any barking or growling, the height and motion of the tail, the lay of the hair at the back of the neck, the position of the head relative to the body, and the exposure of teeth or tongue. In fact, if that movie was really scary, we might think we see all the danger signs even if they aren't actually there. Crazy, right? But true!

> "We shouldn't judge people through the prism of our own stereotypes."
> —Queen Rania of Jordan

Let's imagine that someone stands up to give a talk and sounds to us like a person from another country. Add to this scenario that the speaker is wearing a grass skirt and has tattoos covering his face. Now if this person is talking about an indigenous culture somewhere, then our associations or stereotypes based on how he looks and sounds to us are in harmony with his topic. Therefore, we will be ready to listen. We will assume he knows what he is talking about, and we will be favorably disposed to hear what he has to say. But suppose he begins talking about the issues of urban youth in Los Angeles or gridlock in Washington, DC. We can actually be very distracted by his appearance and our typing of persons with facial tattoos and grass skirts. We can become so distracted that listening to his message will be hard work for us. We might even assume he cannot possibly know what he is talking about.

WE ARE ALL STEREOTYPED

If we take a moment to reflect, we should not be surprised that others have stereotypes of us. Sometimes this works to our advantage. I look Asian, and when I talk, I sound like an educated US-American from the Midwest. When I first meet people or stand up and start giving a talk, there is a general assumption that I am pretty smart. This works to my advantage, because my audience will assume I know what I am talking about, until I stick my foot in my mouth or fail to impress.

Another example of how stereotypes affect us is my daughter, who is half Asian and half white but who is not immediately typed by most people as half Asian. In other words, she often "passes" as white. When people start to get to know her beyond the initial introduction, they become a bit puzzled by her appearance: the closer they look, the more trouble they have trying to categorize her. She plays the violin. Her conclusion is that if people know or suspect she is white, then they think she is a talented musician who works hard. But if people perceive her as Asian, then they think she is talented *and* had a tiger mother (a demanding, success-oriented parent). If people think she is Asian, then there is a bit less respect for her accomplishments and a tinge of pity for her assumed high-pressure childhood.

We might already have ideas about what outsiders think of us. Sometimes we do know, but many times we just think we know. We see things and assume they see things in (excuse the bad pun) black and white, and we fail to create space and develop relationships that will allow us to see one another in full color, as individuals. So in the context of community building, we have to work to recognize and face our stereotypes—positive and negative, ours and theirs. The process of opening up to discussions about stereotypes and of analyzing the power they have in our lives is a core piece of gaining ICQ knowledge. As Mai Chen has noted about the next decades in our multiethnic, multi-cultured realities, "The ability not to stereotype culture and values, but remain open to listening until you really understand who and what you are dealing with will become paramount."

Stereotypes are real. They live in our heads, thrive in our imaginations, are perpetuated in the media, and affect how we think and feel about things in the world. **Stereotypes are *not* reality.** In fact, we cannot acquire the whole truth about any type of thing by reading Wikipedia, or from a single visit, or through a relationship with one example, and we certainly cannot do so from exaggerated stories, single events, misinterpretations, or Hollywood blockbusters. **To get past the stereotypes, we have to explore and learn, stay curious and open to new experiences, and look for those opportunities that help us get to know others and consider their perspectives.** We need to nurture a generous curiosity, purposely peel away those automatic sticky notes, and recognize the stereotypes and "the things we think they think about us" that surround an encounter, pushing them aside as best we can to make space for knowing each other as each wishes to be known. Then and only then is there the hope that different people who are not naturally part of one another's in-group can start to become a community in which people feel as if they belong together.

THE ICEBERG METAPHOR

Gaining knowledge about cultures and how they are put together can help us improve our understanding of ourselves and those from other cultural backgrounds. In this chapter, we are focusing on how we are shaped by our cultures and how we carry with us stereotypes about cultures that affect how we act and react in relation to others. We can understand people and their cultures better if we consider how the products, practices, and perspectives of a culture hang together.

One common way of understanding culture is through the metaphor of an iceberg. The tip of the iceberg above the water represents the pieces of cultures that we can easily see, sometimes referred to as the three F's (food, festivals, and fairy tales) or as heroes and holidays. However, the bulk of what makes a culture lies beneath the surface of the water. Ways of doing things (expectations for behaviors or practices) and values, beliefs, or general views of the world lie below the surface. These elements are more difficult to see clearly, but they are in fact what stabilizes the entire iceberg and determines how it floats in the water. Sometimes these underlying forces are somewhat hidden even from the people in the group.

Figure 2.4. The Iceberg Metaphor
Used by permission

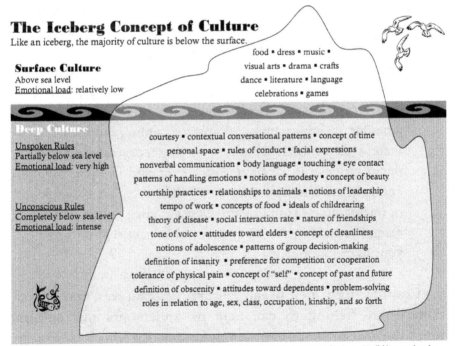

The Iceberg Concept of Culture

Like an iceberg, the majority of culture is below the surface.

Surface Culture
Above sea level
Emotional load: relatively low

food ▪ dress ▪ music ▪
visual arts ▪ drama ▪ crafts
dance ▪ literature ▪ language
celebrations ▪ games

Deep Culture

Unspoken Rules
Partially below sea level
Emotional load: very high

Unconscious Rules
Completely below sea level
Emotional load: intense

courtesy ▪ contextual conversational patterns ▪ concept of time
personal space ▪ rules of conduct ▪ facial expressions
nonverbal communication ▪ body language ▪ touching ▪ eye contact
patterns of handling emotions ▪ notions of modesty ▪ concept of beauty
courtship practices ▪ relationships to animals ▪ notions of leadership
tempo of work ▪ concepts of food ▪ ideals of childrearing
theory of disease ▪ social interaction rate ▪ nature of friendships
tone of voice ▪ attitudes toward elders ▪ concept of cleanliness
notions of adolescence ▪ patterns of group decision-making
definition of insanity ▪ preference for competition or cooperation
tolerance of physical pain ▪ concept of "self" ▪ concept of past and future
definition of obscenity ▪ attitudes toward dependents ▪ problem-solving
roles in relation to age, sex, class, occupation, kinship, and so forth

Indiana Department of Education ▪ Office of English Language Learning & Migrant Education ▪ www.doe.in.gov/englishlanguagelearning

BROAD CULTURES, SUBCULTURES, AND MICROCULTURES

Expanding how we think about cultures (other cultures, cultures in general, and our own cultures) is an important step in building our Interpersonal Cultural Intelligence. Let's take a closer look at a few levels of cultural groupings. There are many definitions for these terms, but we will focus on ones useful for our discussions.

Broad cultures include many people, have long histories, and tend to change slowly. An example of a broad culture is Western culture, referring to cultures with roots in European ideas of enlightenment, the individual as agent and actor in his or her world, and democracy. Broad cultures also include national cultures, such as French culture or Thai culture.

Subcultures are cultural groups within a larger culture or cultures, often having key differences compared to the broader culture(s) of which they are a part. Examples of a subculture are Mormon culture, African American culture(s), and hippies culture. None of the broad cultures or subcultures are homogenous; each is a mosaic of differences, but there are commonalities or generalizations useful for navigating or understanding life in those subcultures.

Microcultures are smaller specialized groups (smaller than a subculture) marked by characteristics, expectations, values, and so on that they claim as their own. Microcultures have a unique identity within a dominant culture, and members share a set of goals, purposes, or perspectives. Sometimes microcultures can be quite local or limited in their influence, purposes, or how long they will be together. Examples of microcultures could be the Westside High School debate team, Fountain Street Church, or the cancer support group your sister just joined.

Considering which broad cultures, subcultures, and microcultures we belong to can help us understand our cultural identities. We might begin by listing for ourselves which cultures are important to our identities, using a grid such as the one in Figure 2.5. (Learning kit activity 2E can help you analyze and reflect more on the different cultures that combine to form your cultural identity.)

Figure 2.5. Breaking Down a Cultural Identity

Which cultures are part of my cultural identity?		
Broad Cultures	Subcultures	Microcultures

THE THREE P'S TOOL FOR ANALYZING CULTURES

There are many ways to define culture, but one particularly useful one for our purposes is the Three P's Tool. (See Figure 2.6.) This tool looks at **culture as a system of products, practices, and perspectives that generally characterize a group.** We can imagine the products as the tip of the iceberg, the food, festivals, and fairy tales or types of things we notice or easily associate with a culture. Connected to that, possibly just below the surface, are the practices. These are the behaviors and etiquette that include rules for being polite, standard procedures or expectations, and common practices for getting along. The bottom or deepest level is summed up by perspectives. This level includes our deepest beliefs or assumptions about how the world works and why, also known as worldview and cultural values.

> "Tolerance, openness, and understanding towards other people's cultures, social structures, values and faiths are now essential to the very survival of an interdependent world."
> —Aga Khan IV

The three P's of products, practices, and perspectives encompass many things. Figure 2.7 provides some examples of what we might find at each level of the triangle.

Figure 2.6. The Three P's Tool for Analyzing Cultures

Products
food,
festivals,
fairy tales

Practices
behaviors
etiquette

Perspectives
worldview
cultural values

Figure 2.7. Examples of Products, Practices, and Perspectives

Products	<ul><li>Burger King whoppers</li><li>thirty-year mortgages</li><li>rugby</li><li>the play *Macbeth*</li><li>hijab or headscarf</li></ul>	<ul><li>incense</li><li>cell phones</li><li>disposable diapers</li><li>Christmas trees</li><li>menorahs</li></ul>
Practices	<ul><li>wearing deodorant</li><li>making charitable donations</li><li>observing Sabbath</li><li>covering your head to pray</li><li>bowing in greetings</li><li>dividing the restaurant bill</li><li>lending money with interest</li></ul>	<ul><li>avoiding eye contact</li><li>eating fish on Fridays</li><li>fasting during Ramadan</li><li>arriving at the digital clock time stated in an invitation</li><li>taking off shoes when entering a home</li></ul>
Perspectives	<ul><li>an adult individual has the right to decide whom to marry</li><li>maintaining the honor of family is very important</li><li>the land is like a mother, so bodies of water near my hometown are part of what defines who I am</li><li>individual accomplishments and productivity are not very important life goals</li><li>all human beings are created equal</li><li>"traditional" is good</li></ul>	

Cultures are systems. The different pieces or levels tend to hang together and affect one another. Let's take another look at the three P's by way of Figure 2.8. In the left column are some examples of the three P's from my home culture. The right column contains descriptions of the connections among these specific products, practices, and perspectives.

Figure 2.8. Connections among the Three P's

Products	<ul><li>fast-food takeout</li><li>calendar apps</li><li>alarm clocks and timers</li></ul>	"Time is of the essence." Getting a quick meal can help me save time for things that are more important. My calendar helps me organize my time. My clocks and alarms help me be on time for work and not go over time when I teach.
Practices	<ul><li>eating lunch while working at my laptop</li><li>clocking in and out</li><li>charging by the hour</li><li>timing my runs</li></ul>	"I just don't have enough time." I am perpetually busy. It takes an online poll to find a meeting time for more than four people because our calendars are full. I try to pack more into my time by multitasking, such as eating lunch while I continue to work, usually food I can get fast. Some people earn money or charge by the hour, like my mom's lawyer, who actually charges by the minute.
Perspectives	<ul><li>I experience time as a limited commodity. (I invest time. I spend time. I measure time carefully.)</li><li>Time is part of the important equation of productivity.</li><li>My productivity is a measure of how valuable I am.</li></ul>	"I invested so much time in that." When I experience failures, the lost time is part of the failure. Sometimes I am sadder about the lost time than about the failure itself. Time is like the denominator in my math formula for productivity. Three books completed or divided by one year is better than one book in three years. My time must be filled with activities that are valuable and, if possible, result in products that are valuable. If I say I have a lot of free time or if I don't continue to do and produce things, I am afraid my boss might wonder if I am doing my job. It is important to me to be seen as productive and as using my time well.

In Figure 2.8 we can see how the products like fast-food and calendar apps enable or are part of the practices of eating quickly to save time and of keeping track of my minutes and hours. Both the products that monitor and "save" time and the practice of tracking my time are linked to key perspectives such as how I relate to or value time as a limited commodity.

> "Most of my important lessons about life have come from recognizing how others from a different culture view things."
> —Edgar H. Schein

Let's dig a little deeper to explore the three P's and to consider how understanding the system or internal logic of one set of products, practices, and perspectives can give us insights into other parts of a culture. Figure 2.9 describes a linked set of three P's in traditional Chinese culture: a product (four hundred distinct terms for family members), a practice (putting a family name before a first name), and a perspective (traditions and elders are valuable).

Figure 2.9: One Three-P's Analysis of "Family" in Chinese culture

The Chinese language has over 400 distinct terms for different family members compared to a couple dozen in most European languages. When you introduce yourself in Chinese, your family name comes first (for example, Smith, Ansari, or Shen) followed by your individual given name (for example, Joe, Ahmed, or Shenghui). In many Asian or Eastern cultures including China, honoring family clans, especially of the father, and showing respect to one's elders is practiced and valued.

PRODUCT: vocabulary, 400 words for family members

PRACTICE: saying and writing the family name before individual or "first" name

PRACTICE & PERSPECTIVE: tradition of high value placed on respect for elders and honoring family clans

In traditional Chinese cultures, multiple generations of a family lived together. Men remained in their family group, while the women left their families to join the clans of their husbands. Members of these family clans took care of one another, and these clans were the social building blocks of society. Since people grew up with the cousins, aunts, uncles, and grandparents on the father's side but might see the cousins, aunts, uncles, and grandparents on the mother's side only occasionally, there were different terms, for example, for an uncle on the mother's side and an uncle on the father's side. Age was also respected, so there were different terms for the paternal uncle older than the father and the paternal uncle younger than him. The distinctions went on and on because hierarchy, family connections, paternal relatives (in contrast to maternal ones), and respect for elders were highly valued in the culture.

Even with this very brief look at one linked set of products, practices, and perspectives in traditional Chinese culture, we might begin to understand better or at least differently how radical China's one-child policy was. Fewer and fewer people have older *and* younger siblings or any sibling at all. Family clans disappeared as the grandparents outnumbered the grandchildren. Perhaps we can even begin to understand better some of the concrete effects on families of having one daughter and no sons. An analyzing tool like the Three P's Tool can help us understand another culture in richer ways.

Building our ICQ knowledge involves learning about the other people in our lives, our schools, our cities, and our world. **The first step to learning about others is to recognize our stereotypes. Then we can start investing the required energy to become more culturally knowledgeable about both ourselves and our neighbors.** The food, festivals, and fairy tales can be part of building our knowledge about cultures, but the things that are visible in a culture are just the surface and may sometimes not even represent the culture appropriately. For example, how many Germans actually wear lederhosen? If our knowledge stops at the food booth, it is pretty shallow. **To be better able to engage across cultural lines, we need to start reflecting on how products, practices, and perspectives link together.** The next chapters will help us further explore some of these connections.

QUESTIONS TO CONSIDER

1. Can you think of one example of a linked product, practice, and perspective from your life or culture(s)?

2. Do the stereotypes associated with you and your assumed cultures mean good or bad things generally for you in your everyday life?

NOTES AND RESOURCES

Quotations in this chapter are taken from David Livermore, *Leading with Cultural Intelligence* (New York: AMACON/Harper Collins, 2015), 64; Henry David Thoreau, *Walden* (New York: Thomas Y. Cromwell, 1910), 8. Queen Rania al Abdullah, "Queen Rania to Fareed Zakaria: 'We need to build channels of communication.'" https://www.queenrania.jo/en/media/interviews/interview-fareed-zakaria-cnn (accessed May 16, 2019); "Aga Khan speaks of tolerance and shared heritage." 2003. https://www.akdn.org/press-release/aga-khan-speaks-tolerance-and-shared-heritage (accessed May 16, 2019); and Edgar H. Schein, *Humble Inquiry. The Gentle Art of Asking instead of Telling* (Oakland, CA: Barrett-Koehler: California, 2013), Chapter 7.

24 **called a *mihi* in the Maori language:** The sample Maori *mihi* greeting is taken from Maori Language Commission, accessed June 3, 2015, http://www.korero.maori.nz/forlearners/protocols/mihimihi.html.

26 **provide the "mental programming":** Culture as mental programming is promoted by Geert Hofstede in his book *Cultures and Organizations: Software of the Mind* (New York: McGraw-Hill Education, 2010). In this book, he defines culture as the collective mental programming of the mind and explains in detail the six cultural orientations overviewed in our chapter 3.

27 **Christena Cleveland:** *Disunity in Christ. Uncovering the Hidden Forces That Keep Us Apart* (Downers Grove, IL: InterVarsity Press, 2013).

29 **Chimamanda Ngozi Adichie:** She is a speaker and author with keen insights into stereotypes and cross-cultural encounters. See her TED Talk "The Danger of a Single Story," accessed October 4, 2018, https://www.ted.com/talks/chimamanda_adichie_the_danger_of_a_single_story?language=en.

30 **Steve Robbins:** He is a public speaker and workshop host who focuses on cognitive flexibility and behavioral adaptability to address racism, diversity, and inclusion issues in organizations and society. His book *What If? Short Stories to Spark Diversity Dialog* (Boston: Nicholas Brealey Publishing, 2009) offers food for thought on these important issues.

30 **our brains are wired to quickly identify insiders and outsiders:** Nobel Prize winner Daniel Kahneman, in his book *Thinking Fast and Slow* (New York: Farrar, Straus and Giroux, 2013) offers research-based explanations of how our brains associate, make choices, and take shortcuts. He argues that the brain jumps to intuitive judgments based on very little information and will make up stories to confirm biases.

30 We might "type" all gray dogs as dangerous: We often react emotionally to and act based on our stereotypes. We might invite, shun, hire, judge, or even shoot a gun because of what we think we see, even if our perceptions are shaded by our stereotypes as much as or more than by reality.

32 We might already have ideas about what outsiders think of us: Social psychologist Christena Cleveland refers to these ideas of what others think of us as "metaperceptions." Her book *Disunity in Christ* offers keen psychology-based insights for both faith-based and non-faith-based intercultural learning.

32 Mai Chen: "NZ Melting Pot Needs Special Cooks," *New Zealand Herald,* June 4, 2015, A29.

32 We need to nurture a generous curiosity: Cleveland points out that we tend toward "cognitive miserliness"; in other words, we tend to categorize people (and ideas and things) as either part of our in-group, which is safe, composed of individuals who are each unique and very human, or part of the out-group, which is in our minds less safe, more homogenous than our in-group, often identified with stereotypes, and in that way less human. It takes a good deal of evidence to psychologically move something from the out-group to our in-group. This is the nature of cognitive miserliness. "Perhaps the most important reason why personal interaction is so valuable in a cross-cultural situation is that it motivates us to see other group members as individuals and provides a natural, ongoing setting in which we can develop friendships. . . . Personal interaction, especially when we are working on a collaborative project, can be just the kick in the pants that we need to be cognitively generous" (Cleveland, *Disunity in Christ*, 172). Cleveland argues for a generous curiosity that she calls "cognitive curiosity."

34 Expanding how we think about cultures: See definitions at https://sociology dictionary.org/.

35 The Three P's Tool: This model is promoted by the American Council on the Teaching of Foreign Languages (ACTFL) for analyzing and understanding cultures, both our own and others. More details can be found at https://www.actfl. org/sites/default/files/pdfs/TLE_pdf/TLE_Apr12_Article.pdf. Additional definitions and examples of products, practices, and perspectives can be found at http:// carla.umn.edu/cobaltt/modules/curriculum/textanalysis/Practices_Products _Perspectives_Examples.pdf

38 In traditional Chinese cultures: Chinese languages and cultures are far more diverse and multifaceted than many in the West realize. The statements about Chinese or Asian or Southeast Asian cultures throughout this book are generalizations. The example of traditional family structures and terms for distinguishing familial relationships is adapted from work by and direct communication with Chinese language teachers and cultural experts Qin Xue Herzberg and Larry Herzberg. See especially the following books by these authors: *Chinese Proverbs* *and Popular Sayings: With Observations on Culture and Language* (California: Stone Bridge Press, 2012) pages 74-77 and *China Smart: What You Don't Know, What You Need to Know—A Past & Present Guide to History, Culture, Society, Language* (California: Stone Bridge Press, 2019) pages 93-96.

Book Suggestion

Michael Fosberg, *Incognito: An American Odyssey of Race and Self-Discovery* (Incognito, Inc. 2011). This book is the true account of a man who grew up white, then discovered as an older adult that his father was African American. We read about his struggles with identity and gain some glimpses into different subcultures. This book has some mature content. His story is also highlighted in this article from the Chicago Tribune: https://www.chicagotribune.com/news/ct-xpm-2013-02-11-ct-met-trice -black-identity-incognito-0211-20130211-story.html.

Film Suggestions

Guess Who's Coming to Dinner (1967) not rated. In this now classic comedy-drama starring Spencer Tracy, Sidney Poitier, and Katharine Hepburn, a young white woman invites her boyfriend over for dinner. Her parents are surprised when their dinner guest turns out to be a black man.

Twelve Angry Men (1957) not rated. A dissenting juror played by Henry Fonda slowly convinces the rest of the jurors that a young person not from the majority culture is not guilty of murder. The classic black-and-white film highlights different perceptions and the power of stereotypes, assumptions, and biases.

Lawrence of Arabia (1962) PG. This classic movie starring many famous actors tells one version of the story of T. E. Lawrence, a controversial figure who played key roles during World War I in the Middle East. Striking in the movie is the depiction of Lawrence's impressive knowledge about the Arab and clan cultures in the region. The real Lawrence did spend years in the Arabian Peninsula and is reported to have taken a keen interest in learning about the local cultures, even visiting workers in their homes. He wrote to his parents, "The foreigners come out here always to teach, whereas they had much better learn" (Scott Anderson, "The True Story of Lawrence of Arabia, Smithsonian.com, July 2014, http://www.smithsonianmag.com/history /true-story-lawrence-arabia-180951857/?no-ist=&page=2).

3

She, He, and They—
ICQ Interpretation

A QUICK LOOK AT THE CHAPTER

This chapter focuses on ICQ interpretation to help us improve our ability to compare and understand the differences between cultures. We will get to know and practice using three tools for understanding how and why people think and do certain things differently from other people. In other words, this chapter introduces three tools to help us interpret cultural practices and perspectives.

- The Three Circles of Cultural Identity Tool helps us consider what is core to our identities, explore ways of understanding differences, and think more flexibly about products, practices, and perspectives.
- The Cultural Dimensions Tool helps us better understand how broad cultures are similar and different.
- The My Guiding Orientations Tool helps us analyze subcultures, microcultures, and our own or others' orientations for navigating everyday life.

Improving flexibility in thinking, understanding differences between broad cultures, and analyzing guiding orientations are skills to help us interpret the actions and reactions of ourselves and others in intercultural situations.

THE THREE CIRCLES OF CULTURAL IDENTITY TOOL

Some teens stay out past curfew. Some stop going to Mass. Some participate in things they shouldn't. Some use language or substances their parents do not approve of. I refused to wear nylons. For cultural reasons, wearing nylons for my mother was linked to ideas of being well-dressed, well-mannered, respectable, polished, and pretty; not wearing nylons to church or fancy restaurants or cultural events was like showing up only partly dressed for the occasion. Bare legs were for yard work, beaches, young children, and people who could not afford nice clothes. My mother and I had more than one argument, especially on hot summer days, about wearing nylons to church. I remember my mother asking me once in desperation, "Would you go bare-legged to see the president?"

When parents and children disagree about faith or curfews or nylons, the clashes have many causes, but one of them is often that the young people are figuring out who they are, pushing the boundaries of the parents' cultures and ideas in order to see where their own personal boundaries might lie. The parents in turn are tracing the boundary lines that they have because those are the definitions of good or right or appropriate or respectable in their cultures and in their minds. Contrary to what children may think, parents are generally not out to be annoying; they are reinforcing their values and norms and giving their children a type of cultural heritage. In some ways, the parents are equipping their children for success or survival in their cultures, as the parents understand or perceive it. Of course, back in the day, I just thought my mother was unreasonable. Who needs to wear nylons in a Michigan summer when it is 95 degrees Fahrenheit and humid? The trick for all of us is determining which pieces of our cultures and identities are central and essential and which are not.

Our identities are comprised of a core set of things that we consider essential to our sense of self or of who we really are. We can use the Three P's Tool from chapter 2 to talk about the products, practices, and perspectives that we would put into this core set of things. A helpful way to visualize our identity is as a set of three concentric circles. (See Figure 3.1.) The circle in the middle represents our essential or central core, the things that really define us: without them we believe we would be very different people. The second or middle circle is filled with the products, practices, and perspectives that we prefer but we can be flexible about; in other words, if we have to, we can give them up or see them as not central to our identity. The outside circle represents the products, practices, and perspectives that we believe are optional or additional to who we are. We can be pretty flexible in how we do or do not integrate these elements into our lives.

Figure 3.1. The Three Circles of Cultural Identity

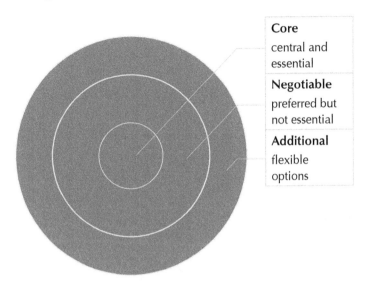

Core
central and essential

Negotiable
preferred but not essential

Additional
flexible options

Long after our teen years, we can find ourselves wondering where the borders of our identities lie, especially where the border between the essential and the negotiable runs. This wondering is an important part of becoming more culturally intelligent. Each culture, each generation, each individual works out which products, practices, and perspectives are core, negotiable, and additional. As many parents and children realize at some point, there are things that we thought were central but are actually pieces of our lives that we can push into the preferred but not essential circle. My mother gave up long ago trying to get me to wear nylons and makeup in a 1950s sort of way. She always wore nylons to church in the summer and never went out in public without makeup (without "her face on"), but she understood that while these practices are important to her identity, they are completely optional parts of my identity. And she was okay with that. Decades after my teen years,

> "The rapproachment of peoples is only possible when differences of culture and outlook are respected and appreciated rather than feared and condemned, when the common bond of human dignity is recognized as the essential bond for a peaceful world."
> —J. William Fulbright

when I had the opportunity to hear the president of the United States speak in person, I wore a skirt and socks (not nylons) and took a bit of pleasure in telling my mother so.

It is important for us to think about what is core and what is negotiable or preferred but not essential. Things can shift over time from one category to another for us as individuals and for the groups or cultures to which we belong. But these facts do not mean that everything is relative. In fact, it is equally important to understand what is truly central to who we are and why. In some cases, practices or perspectives we previously ignored suddenly become important to us. Sometimes the teens who rejected the boundaries of their parents later return and trace those same boundaries for their own children. In any case, if we have thought hard about which things are essential and which products, practices, and perspectives we can be flexible on, we are in a much better position to understand why other people do things and think in ways that seem odd or even unreasonable to us.

THE CASE OF HEADSCARVES

One of today's sometimes controversial cultural practices is the wearing of the hijab or the niqab. The headscarf (hijab) or the scarf-and-face veil that reveals only the eyes (niqab) are worn by some women in certain Muslim cultures or subcultures. In both the East and the West, among Muslims and non-Muslims, we can find men and women for and against this practice. In past years, the issue has become more political. In France, Muslim women choosing to wear the hijab or the niqab have been forced by national laws *not* to wear the head coverings to attend public school. In Canada, they have not been allowed to take the oath of citizenship. Opponents of the hijab often see the cultural practice of wearing head coverings as antidemocratic, unpatriotic, and a practice oppressive to women. At the same time, there are women in the Far East, the Middle East, and the West who choose to wear the hijab or the niqab; the practice is central to their identities as women and Muslims. While ICQ does not give anyone a license to proclaim judgment on cultural practice, it can help us understand both sides of an issue in deeper ways.

In many Western countries, the freedom of the individual and self-determination are core values at the cultural level and therefore also strongly held values for many or most people from those countries. If I feel in the core of my being that I as an individual should be able to choose my religion, my spouse, whether I go to college or to church or wear nylons, then I will react against other people dictating what I am to do in any of those areas. I might easily find that a group of religious leaders mandating that all women wear the niqab is denying the human rights of those women to decide their own fate, to self-determine in such matters as their clothing. Moreover, if my culture is founded on a claim to separate religion and state, I may see the hijab as a religious practice that has no place in matters of state and perhaps even defies or insults the state and its values.

On the other hand, if I wear the hijab as a practice linked to a deeply held religious faith or cultural affiliation, this practice can become part of what is essential to my identity. A Muslim hijab, a Jewish yarmulke, or an Amish simple dress of blue fabric can be much more than things to wear; they can be for certain people product, practice, and perspective all rolled into one. For example, the product of the headscarf and the practice of wearing it can be an act of faith and faithfulness, an important symbol of a person's commitment to their faith and their religious identity. So for these persons of faith, wearing these clothing items can be completely different from my friends in France not being allowed to wear a cross pendant to public school. My friends might wear a cross pendant on Tuesday, a gold chain on Thursday, and a string of pearls on the weekend. The cross is a religious symbol, yes, but wearing it is not a perspective-linked practice that defines their identities. Many hijabis, women who wear the hijab, view this practice as an issue of both faith and cultural affiliation central and essential to who they are.

The hijab controversy is thus radically different from the situation of a teenager in Michigan battling her mother about wearing nylons in the summer. As much as my mother never went to church bare-legged or without her face on, she believed deep down that types of clothing and styles of makeup are negotiable; they may be closer to her core than they are to my core, but they are not the things that are most important and make us who we are or jeopardize our faith. In other words, a cultural practice, such as appropriate clothing, for one group can be seen as negotiable or even additional, while for a different group that same practice is essential. This insight does not negate the fact that some women may be forced to wear the hijab against their will. What is important here is to realize that we have to be very careful when we point a finger at another person or culture to tell them that something they believe is central should be negotiable or optional.

> "We can love what we are, without hating what- and who we are not. We can thrive in our own tradition, even as we learn from others, and come to respect their teachings."
> —Kofi Annan

Distinguishing core, negotiable, and additional practices and perspectives helps us understand other people, perspectives, and cultures. Using the Three Circles of Cultural Identity Tool can build our capacity to interpret cultural practices—the skill set we are exploring in this chapter. Through better understanding of cultural practices and perspectives other than our own, we increase our capacity to have open-minded and open-hearted discussions about cultural differences, about issues that arise when cultures come in contact, about perspectives and practices, including controversial ones.

THE CULTURAL DIMENSIONS TOOL

Our second goal for this chapter is to learn more about how cultures differ by looking at six dimensions of cultures, six key ways that cultures can differ. **Understanding cultural dimensions can help us interpret what is going on in intercultural situations or when we encounter ideas or behaviors that seem strange to us.** After the description of each cultural dimension below, there is a line. On that line, write US, C, and F to mark where you think the USA, China, and France might fall between the two ends of the described cultural dimension.

1. Power distance. How much emotional distance is there between the powerful people (boss, teacher, parent) and the less powerful people (employee, student, child)? Small power distance means the boss can be one of the gang, education might be student-centered, and parents raise children to think for themselves. In large power distance cultures, employees do not question the boss, education is teacher-centered, and children respect and obey their parents and elders on principle.

Small power distance   Large power distance

2. Collectivism versus individualism. What is more important to your identity: the family and groups to which you belong or your individual talents and personality? In a collectivistic society, group harmony should be maintained, and relationships are more important than personal accomplishments, so loyalty to family or tribe is central. In an individualistic culture, voicing your opinion is healthy, and your personal productivity or awards are measures of success.

Collectivism   Individualism

3. Caring versus strength.   Are emotional and social gender roles blended and overlapping or more distinct and well-defined? In caring-oriented cultures, there is a balance between work and family, compassion for the weak is a value, and there are more matter-of-fact attitudes toward sex. In strength-oriented cultures, work prevails over family, the strong are admired, and there tend to be moralistic attitudes about sex.

Caring   Strength

4. Uncertainty avoidance. How tolerant are you of ambiguity or not knowing something? Weak uncertainty avoidance describes a culture in which changing jobs is no big deal, teachers can say "I don't know," and having a lot of rules can be annoying; this culture does not mind uncertainty. In contrast, a culture in which deviate persons or ideas are seen as dangerous and rules are important for keeping order has a strong uncertainty avoidance; this culture wants to avoid uncertainty.

Weak uncertainty avoidance   Strong uncertainty avoidance

←——→

5. Short-term versus long-term orientation. Are you focused on the immediate benefits or willing to delay gratification in hopes of a future gain? Societies with a short-term orientation tend to hold to universal guidelines for good and evil, and students may put the blame for poor performance on luck, teachers, or circumstances. On the other hand, societies with a long-term orientation tend to see good and evil as dependent on circumstances. In long-term oriented cultures, students see their success or failure as a result of their own effort.

Short-term orientation   Long-term orientation

←——→

6. Restraint versus indulgence. Do you think you have control over your life and future? Restraint refers to cultures in which a more fatalistic view prevails, fewer people participate casually in sports, and fewer claim to be very happy people. Indulgence is the label for cultures in which leisure and freedom of speech are important and a higher percentage of people claim to be happy.

Restraint   Indulgence

←——→

Based on significant amounts of survey data, Geert Hofstede and colleagues assigned over seventy countries a number between 1 and 100 for each of these six cultural dimensions. The actual number for a country isn't so important, but the number relative to the numbers of other countries is. **The bigger the difference between two national cultures, the more likely misunderstandings can arise in that area of life.** Here are the results for the three countries we are analyzing: the US, China, and France.

Figure 3.2. Hofstede Cultural Dimensions for the US, China, and France

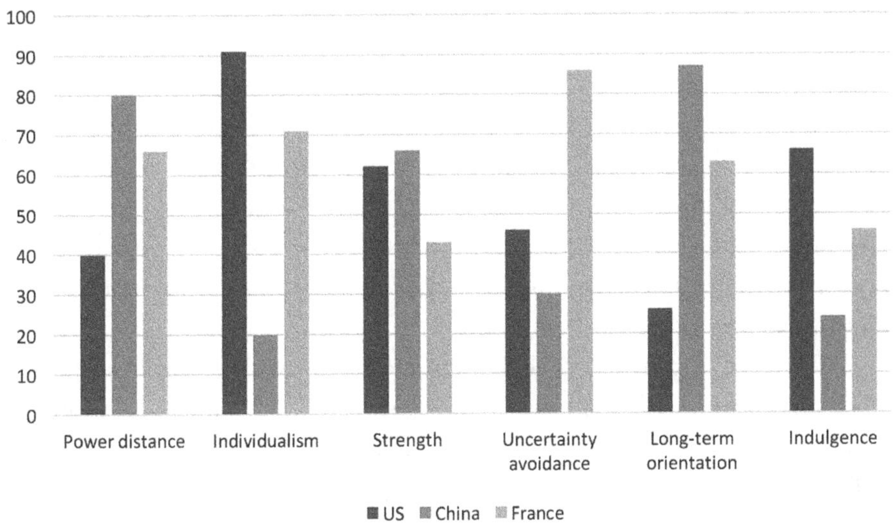

You might be thinking that France and the US are more similar to each other than either is to China. However, the results in Figure 3.2 reveal that this is true only for some dimensions. For example, while the US and France are both much more individualistic than China, for dimensions such as strength and uncertainty avoidance, the US and China are more similar to each other and France is the outsider. For some other dimensions such as power distance and long-term orientation, France and China are more similar to each other and the US is more different. **Understanding these cultural dimensions is not simple. Cultures match up differently on different dimensions, which is one of the reasons why this tool can be useful.** (You can learn more about how cultural dimensions can help you interpret intercultural situations by doing some of the activities in the learning kit.)

> "One of the most effective ways to learn about yourself is by taking seriously the cultures of others."
> —Edward T. Hall

THE CASE OF CHINA'S ONE-CHILD POLICY

Formally introduced in 1979 and phased out in 2015, China's one-child policy called "family planning" was adopted as a temporary measure to address economic problems. In particular, between 1958 and 1962, 30-40 million Chinese died of starvation. Overlapping with this, between 1949 and 1976 the population rose from 550 million to over 900 million, in great part due to the significant increase in life expectancy for most citizens. In 1976, there were so many women of child-bearing age, that the government felt it must do something to curb the trajectory of having too large a population for the country to properly care for.

This family planning policy included incentives for families to have only one child, such as better housing and maternity leave. Birth planning enforcers kept detailed records of women's menstrual cycles, use of contraceptives, and births. While the draconian measures such as mandatory surgery to place a contraceptive device inside women after having a first child and the mandatory sterilization of women after having a second child happened in some cases especially in the first decade, these were not as wide spread as Western media may have led some to believe. In fact, there were many allowed exceptions to the one-child rule and the vast majority of women complied.

In any case, the idea of the government determining in any way how many children a family may have seems contrary to what many of us might think is normal and right. Considering another country's or culture's policies and actions by looking at cultural dimensions can help us see the issues in their cultural context. What is outlined below is a superficial understanding and is not meant to judge the policy, but we can practice trying to understand or interpret what is going on by using one of our cultural interpretation tools—the cultural dimensions.

- China is high on the first cultural dimension, power distance. (China = 80, while the US = 40.) So, in Chinese culture the government, the mayor, the highly educated, the people with power should be respected. What they say goes and should not be questioned much. In contrast, people in the US are more likely to question authority, protest, or engage in acts of defiance.

- China is low on individualism. (China = 20, while the US = 91.) So, in Chinese cultures what I want isn't all that important, but what is best for everyone, society, or the collective is really important. In contrast, people in the US tend to focus on what the individual person wants, what is best for me, and what my rights are.

- China is very high on long-term orientation. (China = 87, while the US = 26.) So, in Chinese culture the one-child policy will help China achieve its desired population by 2080, which was one hundred years in the future at the time the policy was enacted. In contrast, people in the US tend to focus on immediate gains and losses. Politicians want to be reelected in the next couple of years, so a good decision for one hundred years from now is not as important as what will play well to people who will vote them in or out of office at the next election.

- China is low on indulgence. (China = 24, while the US = 66.) So, in Chinese culture freedom of speech, my individual happiness, and personal fulfillment are not what I necessarily expect of the world or what I particularly value. So while I might not like the one-child policy, it is not the same infringement of my rights to personal fulfillment and self-determination as it might seem to someone from the US. In contrast, self-realization, reaching my potential, rugged individualism, and the American dream are important principles for US culture. As a US citizen, I expect the rights of life, liberty, and the pursuit happiness.

Not everyone in China liked or agreed with the one-child policy, but seen or interpreted in its cultural context, the one-child policy is not the dastardly and unimaginable policy in that cultural context that it would be in the US cultural context. The issues related to this policy in China are complex, but considering this idea in light of the cultural dimensions

> "We forget that in most of the world the community still dominates, for without the strength of the community the individual cannot survive. In embracing the cult of the individual, we secure an irresistible sense of liberation and freedom. But it comes at a cost, as is evident in the alienation and isolation that characterizes too many lives in the West."
> —Wade Davis

helps us understand how this could happen. In addition, **seeing how the US and China compare on the different cultural dimensions helps us talk about and understand why we view some issues very differently.** Learning kit activity 3D helps futher explore key differences in US and Asian cultural dimensions.

THE MY GUIDING ORIENTATIONS TOOL

The cultural dimensions above come from research with broad, national cultures. **In contrast, guiding orientations focus more on our personal subcultures and microcultures, the principles or orientations that guide us in our everyday lives.**

Now you get a chance to analyze some of your own guiding orientations with the following self-survey. The survey combines pieces of various models for thinking about how cultures and people are different. Your responses to these guiding orientations may be similar to or different from the cultural dimension results for the broad culture in which you live. Not everyone agrees 100 percent with the values of the broad culture in which they live.

As you work through these questions, you might start to understand the expectations or behaviors you encounter in others. Perhaps you recognize a boss or a coworker at one end of a spectrum and partners from another nation or organization at the other. You might also see yourself at one end of an orientation line and suspect that Uncle George is at the opposite end. (Ah, that explains a lot!)

For each orientation, which phrase (the one on the left or the one on the right) captures best your thinking or orientation? Do you lean toward one end of the spectrum and how strongly? Circle the number that represents where you are on each spectrum. This helps you think about where you are on each orientation, for example: are you more "doing" oriented or more "being" oriented? Do you think your answers are typical for most of the people in your subcultures or micro-cultures? If this type of survey interests you, there is a longer version in the learning kit for chapter 3.

Figure 3.3. My Guiding Orientations Survey (Short Version)

Action: doing or being

Accomplishing a goal or achieving a result is important. Productivity is highly valued.	7 (6) 5 4 3 2 1	The process and experience are more important than a specific accomplishment or product. Relationships are highly valued.

Thinking: linear or systematic

Thinking analytically and breaking problems into small components is key to problem solving.	7 (6) 5 4 3 2 1	Thinking holistically and focusing on the big picture and the inter-relationships among components is key to problem solving.

Communication: instrumental or expressive

An unemotional, imper-sonal communication style is best. Objectivity fosters clear thinking.	7 6 5 (4) 3 2 1	An emotional, personal communication style is best. Subjectivity makes the message real.

Individualism: particular or universal

It is important to consider changing circumstances and personal situations.	7 (6) 5 4 3 2 1	What is true, correct, and appropriate can be identified and applied to everyone. Societal obliga-tions are important.

Social organization: egalitarian or hierarchical

Minimizing differences in level or power or status is a sign of equality and fair-ness. Dwelling on status is elitism (or snobby).	7 6 (5) 4 3 2 1	The status differences between individuals or groups helps maintain clear differences and contributes to an orderly society.

Competitiveness: competitive or cooperative

Achievement, assertiveness, and material success are important. Winning, getting awards, and recognition for individual efforts are good.	7 6 5 4 3 (2) 1	Quality of life, interdependence, and relationships are important. Winning or producing something is not as important as everyone participating and contributing.

You can continue to explore how to interpret intercultural situations and perspectives using the Three Circles of Cultural Identity Tool, the Cultural Dimensions Tool, and the My Cultural Orientations Tool through some of the activities in the learning kit for this chapter.

THE CASE OF AUNTIE PENNY

Once when I visited Cambodia, I got to know Peter, a young college graduate working with a nongovernmental organization (an NGO) in the Cambodian capital Phnom Penh. I knew he was Cambodian and had gotten his bachelor's degree in the US. His family had lived in a couple of different countries besides Cambodia, and his English was excellent. I introduced myself, and after a little back and forth, I encouraged him to call me Penny. He was older than the students I was traveling with and seemed at ease with the suggestion. However, it became clear that he was avoiding using my first name. Finally, at one point on our trip when he couldn't get around it, he blurted out "Auntie Penny" with an apologetic grin. "Is that okay?" he immediately asked. Peter knew that in some US-American cultures, people are more casual and often call each other by first names even across generations. He understood that I had given him permission to call me Penny. But his home culture is high on power distance and low on individualism. Related to that, a guiding orientation for him was that status differences are important and valuable; showing respect for elders or persons with a higher status feels right and good. Not only was I older than Peter, but I was also a professor. So he just couldn't call me by my first name. At a gut level, calling me by my first name just felt disrespectful and wrong.

For Peter, showing respect by calling elders and professors by a title and a family name was in flux: this practice, at least in certain contexts, was moving from something central to his identity to something negotiable. He landed in a middle place, blurting out Auntie Penny as a middle solution. In Cambodian, the word for "aunt" is often used as a sort of title for older women. So calling me Auntie Penny allowed him to show me respect with a title of sorts while honoring my request to be called by my first name.

Peter taught me something important: sensitive compromise. Up until that point in the study trip, the US-American students were also of mixed opinions about how to address the professors. The three professors were fine with first names. Some students found calling them by first names easy; others hesitated. During this trip, we were also constantly engaged with East and Southeast Asians—university students from Korea and Cambodia, local NGO staff, villagers, agency directors, restaurant owners, and political activists. I realized that regardless of what we the US-American professors and our students personally felt about first names (definitely something in the negotiable or additional category), the locals we were engaged with had a different product, practice, and perspective linkage between titles versus first names and showing respect for elders, traditions, and hierarchy. The Korean and Cambodian national cultures are higher on power distance and lower on individualism than US culture. This was also reflected in the individual guiding orientations because showing respect for persons with higher status, including elders and professors, helps maintain social order and reinforces relationships. Showing respect is an obligation. This practice is good and right.

> "The world in which you were born is just one model of reality. Other cultures are not failed attempts at being you; they are unique manifestations of the human spirit."
> —Wade Davis

So the day after Peter asked to call me Auntie Penny, the entire group was told to call the professors Auntie and Uncle. This compromise allowed those of us from the US to create the feeling of approachable friendliness between students and professors that we associate with first names and that we desire because our national culture is lower on the power distance dimension. At the same time, this compromise showed sensitivity to and awareness of the negative gut reactions that our East Asian partners were experiencing by constantly observing the US students casually addressing their professors in a way they felt deep down was disrespectful, no matter what they knew as a fact in their heads.

PUTTING THE TOOLS TO WORK

This brief look at some differences in underlying cultural dimensions and guiding orientations between East and West admittedly glosses over many details and ignores the diversity within these very broad cultural groupings. Nevertheless, **interpretation tools (such as the Three Circles of Cultural Identity Tool, the Cultural Dimensions Tool, and the My Guiding Orientations Tool) can help us interpret or understand differences and what is going on in an intercultural situation**.

- In the case of headscarves, a simplistic, one-sided view might be that headscarves are optional clothing and wearing a headscarf is a symbol of oppression and undemocratic values. A more helpful comparison using ICQ interpretation allows us to see that for some women, wearing a headscarf is a core piece of their identity.
- In the case of China's one-child policy, the simplistic, one-sided view might be that it is unfathomable how an entire society could put up with such a policy and that it denies human rights. Using cultural dimensions, we might understand how the one-child policy was adopted with a long-term orientation to realize advantages for the entire country. The advantages for the collective outweighed the disadvantages for the individuals. The pursuit of happiness, self-fulfillment, and self-determination are not as expected within Chinese cultures in the same way they are in US culture.
- In the case of Auntie Penny, a simplistic, one-sided view might be that Peter did not respect Penny's wish to be called by her

first name. Perhaps he didn't understand the request, or he was stuck in his ways. By using cultural dimensions and guiding orientations, we might see how Penny needed to be more flexible and aware of the different ways of showing respect and of the differing needs to do so.

We can also use ICQ interpretation to understand the domestic and local clashes that happen along racial, ethnic, religious, political, or socioeconomic lines; the things we hear about in international news; or why someone we are interacting with is acting a certain way.

Even if we do not have enough information to make profound judgments about everyday or internationally significant events, with better knowledge and interpretation, we might have the ability to ask better questions. We might also be better able to interpret the responses we receive.

QUESTIONS TO CONSIDER

1. Can you provide an example from your life or your family or your community in which something that was central to your identity shifted to be negotiable or something that was negotiable or additional became much more important to who you are?

2. Considering your responses to the guiding orientations survey in Figure 3.3, where do you place yourself in relation to the broader national culture(s) around you? Are your guiding orientations in harmony or at odds with the cultural dimensions of your national culture(s)?

NOTES AND RESOURCES

Quotations in this chapter are taken from Tom Healy, "Remembering Senator J. William Fulbright." *Huffington Post,* June 9, 2018. https://www.huffpost.com/entry /remembering-senator-j_b_3041509; Kofi Annan, Nobel lecture, December 10, 2001. https://www.un.org/press/en/2001/sgsm8071.doc.htm; Edward T. Hall, *Understanding Cultural Differences* (Yarmouth, MA: Intercultural Press, 1990), 136; Wade Davis, interview by Alex Chadwick, *Radio Expeditions,* NPR, May 2003, https://www.npr.org /programs/re/archivesdate/2003/may/mali/davisinterview.html (accessed May 17, 2019); and Wade Davis, cited in Cindy L. Griffen and Jennifer Emerling Bone, *Invitation to Human Communication, 2nd ed.* (Boston: Cengage Learning, 2017), 294.

45 The Three Circles of Cultural Identity: Using these elements of identity is an adaptation of the core versus flex model of Julia Middleton's framework of CQ. See https://commonpurpose.org/knowledge-hub-archive/all-articles/what-is-cultural-intelligence/.

48 In France, Muslim women choosing to wear the hijab: For a comparison of the French and US approaches to headscarves see "The Headscarf: Islam's Gift to Western Democracy," by Matthew Kaemingk accessed October 31, 2018, https://www.cardus.ca/comment/article/the-headscarf-islams-gift-to-western-democracy/.

50 six dimensions of cultures: They can be organized and characterized in many ways. Hofstede's model is only one model, but it is widely known. Country comparisons using Hofstede's rubric can be obtained on this website: https://www.hofstede-insights.com/product/compare-countries/.

51 Caring versus strength: In Hofstede's work, this dimension is labeled feminine versus masculine. Because these terms are loaded with other meanings and uses, the terms "caring" and "strength" are used instead in this book.

56 key differences in US and Asian cultural dimension: Differences in cultural dimensions between East and West have been analyzed by many experts, including Richard Nisbett in his book *The Geography of Thought: How Asians and Westerners Think Differently and Why* (New York: Free Press, 2003). This book is an excellent introductory comparison of Eastern and Western cultures.

Book Suggestion

Anne Fadiman, *The Spirit Catches You and You Fall Down: A Hmong Child, Her American Doctors, and the Collision of Two Cultures* (New York: Farrar, Straus and Giroux, 1997). This book tells the story of a Hmong child with epilepsy and the cultural misunderstandings that happened between the Hmong family and individuals working in the US health care system. The story highlights how cultural orientations and values affect behaviors and interpretation. This narrative underscores our need to learn more about what others truly believe and why.

Film Suggestion

Arranged (2007) not rated. "*Arranged* centers on the friendship between an Orthodox Jewish woman and a Muslim woman who meet as first-year teachers at a public school in Brooklyn. Over the course of the year, they learn that they share much in common—not least of which is that they are both going through the process of arranged marriages" (IMDb).

4

Me and You—
ICQ Interpersonal Skills

A QUICK LOOK AT THE CHAPTER

Interpersonal skills are a key component of intercultural skills. This is good news, because it means that as we use ICQ for community building, we are also improving our ability to interact with all people.

This chapter explores how we can improve our capabilities to communicate and interact on a personal level with people who are a little or a lot different from us. It outlines four interpersonal skills, aligns them with the skills and tools from previous chapters, and considers how ICQ knowledge and ICQ interpretation skills and tools can help us be more personable as we dialogue and interact across lines of difference.

BEING PERSONABLE

We often become most aware of interpersonal skills when we encounter someone who doesn't seem to have them. My student Liam was an example. He was smart and always did his homework. He also pointed out to his classmates that their answers were less than perfectly correct, that they were lazy for not having done all their homework, and that he didn't like working with people who were not as smart or as diligent as he was. He would blurt out comments when a question or a piece of information seemed dumb or irrelevant to him. And he would sigh loudly, roll his eyes, or drum his fingers on the table when another student asked a question he felt was unnecessary. The other students were remarkably gracious. They tried to work in small groups with Liam and took turns bearing the brunt of his somewhat caustic comments.

Liam had not been diagnosed with autism or Asperger's, and, overall, he was a high-functioning student; in terms of his grades and coursework, he was successful. But he lacked interpersonal skills. He failed to observe or read how his peers reacted to him. He did not adjust his expectations of student behaviors so that he could understand or have some openness to student habits and levels of intelligence that were different from his own. He did not show sympathy or empathy for students who were not as smart as he was or who had different priorities than he had. His classroom world and how he functioned in it were defined narrowly by his way of doing things, by his abilities and expectations of how things should be. In some ways, Liam's (dis)ability in regard to interpersonal skills is like our disability in regard to intercultural situations when we do not work to improve our ICQ. We end up limiting ourselves or defaulting to one way of seeing the world, one way of being and acting in it.

While some of us may struggle to engage with people or to enjoy social situations that involve many people, most of us are able to function reasonably well for our social needs. That is true until we are faced with a new situation, another culture, political or religious opinions that we have a really hard time understanding, or even our son's unusual girlfriend. **Building up our interpersonal skills can help us cross all kinds of cultural lines:** those we find in families, workplaces, or schools and those between and among different generations, religions, or national and ethnic cultures or subcultures. So let's examine four interpersonal skills for ICQ.

FOUR INTERPERSONAL SKILLS FOR ICQ

In the popular sitcom *The Big Bang Theory*, the character Sheldon has a unique set of social and intellectual abilities. Although he is a scientific genius and child prodigy, Sheldon lacks a filter on his comments; he is a fanatic about cleanliness, germs, and avoiding unnecessary physical contact; and he demands strict scheduling of his days and habits. But one recurring thing that Sheldon does almost right is this: when someone is feeling sad, he offers them a hot drink. His mother taught him that this is appropriate, and he tries occasionally to do the socially appropriate thing, even if he feels that doing so is actually a little silly. Sheldon's social failures provide many of the funny moments for the show, but his habit of offering a hot drink to anyone he perceives as sad is also in some ways funny. Hot drinks are his cure-all, even if it is a cup of bouillon from a crusty old cube he found in the back of the cupboard.

This chapter does not provide superficial cure-alls for our interpersonal shortcomings. But by focusing on some interpersonal skills, we can become better able to interact well and understand what is going on in all types of interpersonal situations, especially across cultural lines.

There are many ways to define interpersonal skills. In this chapter, **we are focusing on a small set of skills that are learnable; in other words, most of us can become more aware of and actually practice these skills, improving our overall abilities to interact with different people.** Let's begin with an overview of four interpersonal skills for ICQ.

Figure 4.1. Overview of Four Interpersonal Skills for ICQ

Openness	Get your head and heart in open mode. Be willing to learn about others, to listen to their stories, and to grow or change.
Observation	Look at, read about, and explore parts of the cultures or subcultures you hope to or have to engage with. Research the facts. Take notes. Consider how you are reacting and try to figure out why.
Flexibility	Determine which things are central to your identity and improve your flexibility in dealing with others by considering which parts of your identity could move from the core to the negotiable or from the negotiable to the additional category.
Empathy	Explore why people do and believe things differently than you do. Seek to understand an issue or the world from their perspective. Look for commonalities.

Let's continue to unpack each of these interpersonal skills a bit more, linking each skill to the key ideas and tools from the previous chapters.

Openness is a purposeful attitude adjustment. It takes little effort to keep doing what we do, what feels natural or normal. Since you have made it to chapter 4, you probably have a good start on being open. Keep in mind that openness is easy for some and hard for others. Many young children shy away from foods they do not recognize. This is a type of safety mechanism. In fact, avoiding foods we don't recognize makes some sense. After all, they could be poisonous! And yet some children are willing to try anything. I had one of each. My oldest child avoided all fruits and vegetables. All those bright colors and odd textures—who knew what they would do to your tummy! In contrast, my youngest at age three ate salad with gusto. My unofficial parent polls indicate that the adventurous three-year-old eater is probably the unusual one. Unless something about our intercultural encounters is inherently dangerous, we need to encourage one another toward openness, because most of us are probably more like the cautious eater.

> "If you cannot be open-minded, then you do not possess your ideas, your ideas possess you."
> —Bryant McGill

You may be thinking that openness is an attitude, not a skill. But figuring out how to work on this attitude—encouraging ourselves and others to do so—is a skill we can improve. **When we work together with others to recognize and admit the stereotypes that are everywhere and inside our heads, we can get better at being able to listen to and understand people from the other side of town, the other side of the aisle, the other side of the world.** Openness is also like "tuning in" or becoming more aware of the issues. As with other skills, practicing is helpful. We need to create opportunities to practice openness. Consider how your ICQ book group, your organization, or your family can reflect or radiate openness. The chapter 4 learning kit has some ideas to get you started.

Observation is active but not aggressive: look, research, reflect, analyze. When actor Aamir Khan in his forties had to play a university student in the film *The Three Idiots*, he relied on method acting. In particular, he analyzed his teenage son, looking for behaviors, facial expressions, ticks, or ways of doing and being that seemed appropriate or normal for that age group. He adopted several, including the nervous tick of stroking the strap of his book bag, based on observations of his son.

The trick to observation as an interpersonal skill is observing while resisting the urge to judge. We can observe that someone wears clothes in a certain way, has tattoos of a certain type, has an airbrushed makeup look, or wears a hijab. But can we make these observations without immediately slapping a stereotype onto someone? (He must be in a gang; she is so materialistic; they must be ultraconservatives.) **Divorcing observation from judgment takes practice**. Remember how our brains are practically wired to categorize things?

We have to be aware of this tendency in ourselves, peel away the sticky note labels we assign to others, and admit and unpack the stereotypes that auto-fill our thinking.

Good observation involves paying attention and asking good questions: how, when, who, what, why. After all, **observation is part of the journey of trying to understand others.** A while back, a colleague and I met up in O'Hare Airport with a Korean friend in his eighties. We chatted about how our families were doing and touched base on our common projects overseas. Later that day, my colleague said to me, "I noticed that you looked at the ground a lot when we were talking to Seo-jun." I was stunned. First, I was surprised that my colleague had noticed and mentioned it to me.

Then I replayed the encounter in my head. Yes, I had looked at the ground a lot and not into the face of our Korean friend. I sort of remembered choosing to do so but not really. I had just looked at the ground because doing so felt right. You ought to know that although I spent my early childhood in Taiwan, I grew up in the US, in a majority culture family, and grew into adulthood in a university culture. In all those subcultures, a person makes eye contact to show they are listening. But in my interaction with Seo-jun, I looked away because doing so felt more respectful. I *was* listening, but I was showing with my body language that I understood my lesser status, being half his age among other things. (Remember the comparisons in chapters 2 and 3 of some cultural dimensions of Western versus Asian cultures and some guiding orientations for individuals from those cultures.) The point here is not that I adapted my behaviors to fit different cultural expectations, often called code-switching. The point of this story is my colleague's observation skills. He noticed what I had done, and then he asked questions and listened carefully to understand what he had observed.

> "If we are open only to discoveries which will accord with what we know already, we may as well stay shut."
> —Alan Watts

We tend to observe or see products or practices, things that are near the surface in the iceberg metaphor from chapter 2. We notice that someone is wearing a hijab or that someone is avoiding eye contact.

But the next step in building observation skills is to ask questions and to seek to understand what we are noticing in its bigger context. We can dig deeper to see the links between products, practices, and perspectives in the broad cultures or subcultures involved using the Three P's Tool from chapter 2. (Look for ways to practice this skill in the chapter 4 learning kit.)

Flexibility is the skill of adjusting what we do and how we act or react in situations, especially when our default or automatic reactions do not help us engage productively with others. Part of this skill involves learning what is appropriate or expected in certain interactions and in certain cultural settings.

One common, sometimes daily, social event in parts of Germany is the *Kaffeestunde*, or coffee time. Often late in the afternoon, coffee (or tea in the northwest) is served with some type of sweet. Among most of my German acquaintances, decaffeinated coffee is not a household staple. Since I know that caffeinated coffee will likely be served in the late afternoon and since I want to participate and accept this hospitality for what it is, I actually prepare. Prior to my trips to Germany, I purposefully up my daily dose of caffeine, building up my tolerance for a cup of java later in the day.

Here is how I use the Three Circles of Cultural Identity Tool to help me think about this. I gave up large doses of caffeine with my first pregnancy decades ago. Now I admittedly look askance at certain members of my family who are without a doubt addicted. (You know who you are!) Still, when preparing to go to Germany, I allow myself to get hooked just a little. I can be flexible on the caffeine issue. Being reliant on caffeine to start my day is something I avoid. Usually, avoiding being addicted to unnecessary substances is a core or maybe a negotiable part of my identity. But when I am looking forward to cozy coffee times with my German friends, I push the caffeine issue into the additional category of who I am.

So we have to do our homework. We have to learn about appropriate behaviors, taboos, specific rules of etiquette, expectations for social interactions, how other people show respect, and what makes them feel welcome or how they extend hospitality. But **the interpersonal skill of flexibility does not mean just learning lists of do's and don'ts. Rather, we have to tune in to where the differences might be and be willing and able to adjust at least a little bit concerning what we usually do or what we think of as normal or comfortable or proper.**

In some ways, flexibility is like choosing unselfishness for the sake of getting along and building relationships. Examples of flexibility are all around us:

- a father showing an interest in the new video game his daughter is keen on, perhaps even having a go at the controller, even though he generally thinks computer games are a waste of time
- cooking a meat-free thanksgiving dinner because your son invited his vegetarian roommate from college
- taking your Aunt Millie to a Southern gospel concert even though you don't like that style of music

We do these things because we love these people in our lives. Our relationships are worth the effort, inconvenience, time, or money.

Thinking about flexibility as a skill for interpersonal communication with people outside our tight circles and as part of the broader ICQ skills for community building is a modest next step.

- a praise-song type of worshiping community purposely choosing some old hymns because they know some of their expected attendees really like them
- a predominantly white majority culture organization asking how members might partner with a neighboring Hispanic community in their celebrations of *Día de los Muertos*, even though doing so will cost resources and the whole idea of the holiday seems foreign
- making the time to listen to the stories and the reports from the other side of issues; in fact, making this a habit

Taking the time to listen to those whose cultural identities are different from our own creates space to nurture the fourth interpersonal skill: empathy.

Empathy involves understanding the personal "why" of others' actions and perspectives in both a head and a heart way. Sometimes we think of empathy as feeling the same feelings as another person: I can really empathize with someone who just lost a parent, because my father died recently. But empathy in the context of ICQ skills is not just understanding and feeling what someone else is going through because we have gone through the same thing or because we can easily imagine doing so. ICQ empathy is appreciating and understanding other values, stories, experiences, and opinions even when they are not at all like our own. Let's face it. It can be really hard to understand why Aunt Millie voted the way she did, or the other side of the gun law debate (whichever side is different from your own), or how James can feel as if he has been treated unfairly.

"Seek first to understand, then to be understood."
—Stephen Covey

Sociologist Christena Cleveland explains that any cohesive group can fall prey to "The Gold Standard Effect"—thinking that our way of doing things is the right way. This thinking underscores the lines between Us & Them, an in-group and an out-group. Reporting the work of other sociologists, Cleveland argues that focusing on shared characteristics can significantly reduce the us-versus-them mentality.

A shared characteristic could be that we are both Jewish or from North Africa or grew up on the south side of Chicago. But a shared characteristic can also be something that arises from a more nuanced understanding of how our broad cultures, subcultures, and microcultures affect our identities. My brother-in-law loves triathlons and competes in Ironman competitions. In comparison, I am an intellectual couch potato. In my subcultures and microcultures, good ideas are more important than PRs (personal records), brains beat brawn, and published books are cherished over podium medals. We would each fail if we applied our "awesome person" criteria to each other. However, I can appreciate or better understand my brother-in-law's passion for triathlons when I analyze that passion and investment of time and energy by using some of the ICQ tools. Using the Cultural Dimensions Tool, I can see that his commitment to fitness training and competitions is consistent with valuing personal awards or accomplishments, strength, and personal fulfillment. (See the cultural dimensions of strength, individualism, and indulgence in chapter 3.) Using the My Guiding Orientations Tool, I can note that he is probably doing-oriented and competitive, while I am slightly more being-oriented and cooperative. When I use these same tools to analyze myself, suddenly what my brother-in-law and I have in common comes into focus. We both embrace the next challenge or project, we are self-motivated to do our best, we value working consistently over the long haul to achieve personal goals, and we value individual achievements.

Good listening has been described like this: "Listening is not waiting to talk." In a similar way, empathy is not waiting to tell others about our grief, experiences, and opinions. **Empathy, like all the interpersonal skills, is not necessarily a two-way street: we can be empathetic toward someone who does not seem at all interested in empathizing with us.** The interpersonal skill of empathy means we are willing to listen sincerely to the stories and opinions of people on the other side of the issues—the ones we are passionate about and the ones that others care deeply about but we haven't given much thought to. As I try to improve my interpersonal skills, I will ask my brother-in-law about his training, his next competition, and his latest success. I will do this with real interest and admiration for how he embraces challenges, pushes himself, sets goals, and achieves them. I would do this even if he never asked me about any of the books I have written.

> "There are two kinds of people in the world—those who walk into a room and say, 'There you are' and those who say, 'Here I am.'"
> —Pauline Phillips
> ('Dear Abby')

ICQ: THE BIG PICTURE

Let's take a few steps back to see the big picture. How do ICQ interpersonal skills, ICQ knowledge, and ICQ interpretation relate to one another? Figure 4.2 helps us review the key ideas and tools from chapters 1–4 and see some of the connections. For example, understanding stereotypes helps us practice openness. We can build our observation skills by looking at cultural identities using the Three P's Tool and the Cultural Dimensions Tool and by analyzing the broad cultures, subcultures, and microcultures. We can work on our flexibility by using the Three Circles of Cultural Identity Tool to better understand ourselves and others, and to consider where we can try or practice being flexible. And we can work on empathy using the My Guiding Orientations Tool to become more aware of differences and similarities between "us" and "them."

Figure 4.2. Connecting Knowledge, Interpretation, and Interpersonal Skills

ICQ Knowledge	ICQ Interpretation	ICQ Interpersonal Skills
stereotypes		openness
cultural identities	Cultural Dimensions Tool	
Three P's Tool broad cultures, subcultures, and microcultures		observation
	Three Circles of Cultural Identity Tool	flexibility
	My Guiding Orientations Tool	empathy

The links or rows in the table do not mean that one tool is only good for one thing. We can blend and combine the tools and the big ideas and the skills. **One of the big advantages of ICQ for community building is that we develop a common vocabulary so that we can discuss intercultural issues in more depth.** In these creative, constructive conversations with one another and through intentional relationship building across cultural lines, we create connections. We become attached. "They" become part of our "we." The fabric of our society or our community becomes more tightly woven, stronger, and better.

DISCOVERING HOW

You may be wondering, *Interpersonal skills are culturally bound, right? So how do I really figure out how to act and react?* For example, it does little good for me to be friendly by patting your child on the head if in your culture that behavior is seen as defiling something sacred. My Thai friends may know that in the US, patting a child's head is an affectionate gesture, but deep down inside the act can still feel off-putting. (Remember Peter's need to call me Auntie Penny?) Again, ICQ interpersonal skills begin with openness. You are already part of an ICQ for community building group, and you are asking great questions. Remaing curious and asking good questions are key to learning.

Yes, specific expectations for interacting with people are culture- and context-specific. Appropriate body language, communication styles, the "right" words are all bound up with our cultures, languages, and situations. ICQ interpersonal skills are not a list of do's and don'ts. Instead, **ICQ skills provide a way of figuring out and improving how we can engage personally across lines of differences.** The key is discovering how. **ICQ *interpersonal* skills are not the road map to successful intercultural relationships; rather, these skills help us to discover, create, and read those road maps.**

ICQ interpersonal skills help us accomplish three key things:

- be open and observe well
- be flexible as we navigate the role of our cultural identities in our relationships across lines of difference
- show respect and empathy for others

In short, when we improve our interpersonal skills, we are capable of being more personable to more people, including people different from us. ICQ interpersonal skills enable us to understand our differences in helpful ways. Exactly how one expresses things such as respect, kindness, or openness to another person depends on many factors, including cultural dimensions, guiding orientations, and personalities, plus the written and unwritten social rules of the cultures with which we are dealing. **ICQ interpersonal skills help us relate directly with other people, to navigate the uncertainties and look for workable solutions in informed ways**.

TOWARD DIALOGUE

The current cold civil war in the US—the divisions along race and politics—is marked in some cases by fierce debates, often hateful and hurtful. In other cases, people on each side wave their banners and slogans; they tweet and message and post with no real interaction, connection, or relationship with the other side. **ICQ interpersonal skills are a foundation for a positive shift from the debate and banner-waving approaches to dialogue. Dialogue is about change—not a change in you so that you think like me but rather a change in each of us so that we understand our differences in more helpful ways and can describe and compare how we see things and why.** That sounds like a goal of ICQ! So Interpersonal Cultural Intelligence can help us engage across lines of difference, not only between China and the US but also between liberal and conservative, black and white, and rural and urban and new urban.

"I am convinced that men hate each other because they fear each other. They fear each other because they don't know each other and they don't know each other because they don't communicate with each other...."
—Martin Luther King Jr.

One of the trends in universities and certain organizations is to pursue some training in dialogue. Sometimes this training has a social justice agenda. Sometimes it involves one side trying to convince the other side who is right. Sometimes dialogue training is just the next trend in diversity training: we have to keep doing things to try to fix our divisions and deal with the fallout of our differences.

The goal of good dialogue is to listen to and understand others, as opposed to winning a debate or convincing someone that we are right. ICQ for community building is not the last word on dialoging, but we can learn about and use ICQ, especially the interpersonal skills for interaction and dialogue, to communicate with and understand others. ICQ like diversity, inclusion, and dialogue work is about engaging across lines of difference, building our awareness and skills so we can better negotiate life together. (Learning kit 4 has some activities to practice interpersonal skills for interaction and dialogue.)

QUESTIONS TO CONSIDER

1. How do you show respect to people at work? How would you go about discovering or creating a road map to show respect to a new in-law, a boyfriend's grandparents, the parents or guardians of the children in the neighborhood school, or neighbors from a faith tradition different from your own?

2. In many cultures, one way to show respect is to invite the other person to speak. In many cultures and subcultures, if one person hogs all the airtime, we tend to think they are arrogant or bullish or annoying. Can you recall being in an interactive social space with an airtime hog? How did you feel? If you cannot recall any such situation, you may want to observe and consider if that conversation monopolizer tends to be you.

3. In sociolinguistics, we sometimes talk about "turn taking" in conversations. Some people are great at listening and inviting others to share information, stories, and insights or questions. These people must learn to balance their inviting and questioning so that they are perceived as caring and good listeners and not as nosey gossips. What could you do to balance the listening and the speaking by different people at your next family gathering? What would be an appropriate ideal balance for your group or microculture? How might you help the group evolve from where the balance is now to where the ideal would be?

NOTES AND RESOURCES

Quotations in this chapter are taken from Bryant McGill's twitter account, May 7, 2015, 1:44 am. https://twitter.com/bryantmcgill/status/596234198878461952; Alan Watts, *The Wisdom of Insecurity: A Message of an Age of Anxiety* (New York: Vintage Books, 1951), 103; Stephen R. Covey, title of Habit 5 from *The 7 Habits of Highly Effective People: Restoring the Character Ethic* (New York: Simon and Schuster, 1989); Reuters, "Factbox: Advice

from 'Dear Abby' columnist Pauline Phillips," accessed May 16, 2019, https://www
.reuters.com/article/us-dearabby-paulinephillips-quotes/factbox-advice-from-dear
-abby-columnist-pauline-phillips-idUSBRE90G19420130117; and Martin Luther
King, Jr.' Speech, Cornell College, October 15, 1962. "Dr. Martin Luther King's visit to
Cornell College." Cornell College. https://news.cornellcollege.edu/dr-martin-luther
-kings-visit-to-cornell-college/, accessed May 17, 2019.

65 Interpersonal skills are a key component of intercultural skills: Alvino
Fantini is an intercultural education expert. His article on developing intercultural
competence and several conference presentations underscore the importance of
interpersonal skills in intercultural competence. Fantini is also a strong proponent
of the role of language learning in improving our intercultural competence. Fantini outlines key interpersonal skills in his article "A Central Concern: Developing
Intercultural Competence," accessed October 31, 2018, http://www.brandeis.
edu/globalbrandeis/documents/centralconcern.pdf.

67 There are many ways to define interpersonal skills: Emotional Intelligence
and Social Intelligence are also used to talk about interpersonal skills. Google
defines Emotional Intelligence as "the capacity to be aware of, control, and express
one's emotions, and to handle interpersonal relationships judiciously and empa-
thetically." Psychologist Daniel Goleman outlines these key elements of Emotional
Intelligence: self-awareness, self-regulation, motivation, empathy, and social skills.
See "Emotional Intelligence," MindTools, accessed October 31, 2018, https://www
.mindtools.com/pages/article/newCDV_59.htm. Social Intelligence is our ability
to get along well with others and to get them to cooperate with us. A short introduction to Social Intelligence can be found in several spots online, including Ronald E.
Riggio, "What Is Social Intelligence? Why Does It Matter?" *Psychology Today*,
July 1, 2014, https://www.psychologytoday.com/blog/cutting-edge-leadership/
201407/what-is-social-intelligence-why-does-it-matter. A somewhat longer and
very helpful introduction can be found in Daniel Goleman and Richard E. Boyatzis,
"Social Intelligence and the Biology of Leadership," *Harvard Business Review*, Sep-
tember 2008, https://hbr.org/2008/09/social-intelligence-and-the-biology-of
-leadership. The four interpersonal skills outlined in chapter 4 were chosen to
bridge the current work in Social and Emotional Intelligence with the emphases
of Cultural Intelligence.

68 "tuning in": Tuning in to a situation or a context and being aware or mindful of
specific traits of a group or of persons in the group can help reduce the harm or
exclusion that occurs in groups. See Eric E. Jones, et al., "Who Is Less Likely to Ostra-
cize? Higher Trait Mindfulness Predicts Inclusionary Behavior," Sage Journals, June
25, 2018, http://journals.sagepub.com/doi/pdf/10.1177/0146167218780698.

68 When actor Aamir Khan: The story about observing his son is taken from the extra materials on the DVD *The Three Idiots* (California: Twentieth Century Fox Home Entertainment LLC, 2011).

71 *Día de los Muertos*: Día de los Muertos is a three-day Mexican holiday during which family and friends come together to remember and honor loved ones who have died. Central activities include building colorful altars that reference favorite foods and activities, and visits to the cemetery complete with picnics to spend time with the deceased and wish them well on their continued spiritual journey.

72 Christena Cleveland: *Disunity in Christ: Uncovering the Hidden Forces That Keep Us Apart* (Downers Grove, IL: InterVarsity Press, 2013).

76 The goal of good dialogue: See the Program on Intergroup Relations at the University of Michigan, www.igr.umich.edu. More in-depth description and analyses of dialogue and specifically the Intergroup Dialogue approach to dialogue can be found in *Dialogue across Difference: Practice, Theory and Research on Intergroup Dialogue* by Patricia Gurin, et al. (New York: Russel Sage Foundation, 2013). A substantial collection of short texts on various topics related to good dialogue and social justice issues can be found in *Readings for Diversity and Social Justice* edited by Maurianne Adams, Warren J. Blumenfeld, Carmelita (Rosie) Castaneda, Heather W. Hackmand, Madeline L. Peters, and Ximena Zuniga (New York/London: Routledge, 2013).

Book Suggestion

Mark Goulston, *Just Listen* (New York: AMACOM, 2010) provides a great approach and concrete tips for learning to listen well.

Film Suggestions

"*x+y*" released as *A Brilliant Young Mind* in the US (2014) PG-13. This film tells the story of an autistic boy who is a math genius. He, his mother, and others in his life must navigate how to manage the boy's autism (his abilities and disabilities) in the real world.

Inside Out (2015) PG. "After young Riley is uprooted from her Midwest life and moved to San Francisco, her emotions—Joy, Fear, Anger, Disgust, and Sadness—conflict on how best to navigate a new city, house, and school" (IMDb). In this animated, family-friendly movie, viewers explore the advantages and disadvantages of different emotions or approaches to challenging situations. The film can prompt discussion on personality types, biases for certain approaches, and interpersonal skills.

TV Suggestion

The Big Bang Theory was a long-running sitcom. The various characters demonstrate different levels of Emotional and Social Intelligence, which can be interesting prompts for discussion. "The Misinterpretation Agitation," season 8, episode 7, contains examples of Sheldon's "hot drink" solution to awkward social situations.

5

Working on Us—Acting, Reacting, and Our Overall Approach

A QUICK LOOK AT THE CHAPTER

This final chapter considers how we act and react to and approach intercultural situations and cultural differences. We consider strategies for and attitudes toward ICQ and community building. And we conclude with several insights for navigating and thinking about how and why we interact with different people and perspectives.

CULTURAL UPBRINGING

> eleventh juror (rising): "I beg pardon, in discussing . . ."
>
> tenth juror (interrupting and mimicking): "I beg pardon. What are you so goddam polite about?"
>
> eleventh juror (looking straight at the tenth juror): "For the same reason you're not. It's the way I was brought up." (Reginald Rose, *Twelve Angry Men*)

This American theater piece plays out in a jury room where twelve men have to decide whether someone is guilty or innocent of murder. Even in these few lines, we can sense that tensions are high. Under the stress, the eleventh man, a European-born watchmaker, and the tenth man, a garage owner—each with his different ways of doing things—are starting to get on each other's nerves. In my mind, the key difference between them is not that one is polite and the other is not. The key difference is that the watchmaker (whatever he might think about the others in the room) recognizes that the men tend to act in certain ways because that is what their cultural backgrounds taught them.

Politeness is not what one culture has and another does not. Politeness can actually be understood and acted out very differently in different cultures, sometimes in almost opposite ways. The same hand signal can mean okay in one culture and something obscene in another culture. Wearing shoes in the home can be perfectly normal for my father-in-law in the US and an insult to my friend in Bangkok. Making direct eye contact with a US manager who is talking to me shows that I am interested, honest, and respectful, while that same behavior in some Asian contexts could indicate disrespect. Leaving a small amount of soup in my bowl indicates to my Chinese host that he has generously given me more than enough to eat, while a British host might feel that I did not enjoy the meal.

ASK, REFLECT, ADAPT

Even when we have done our homework and know some of the expectations or rules of behavior, doing everything "right" is not necessarily easy. When Eduardo invited me for coffee, he met me at my office, and we walked in the rain to a café across campus. Under his umbrella, we bumped elbows and shoulders but managed to arrive pretty dry. We sat next to each other on a sofa. I learned that he had moved from Latin America to North America to New Zealand for personal reasons and that he enjoyed his job. Our chat was cordial and pleasant.

On our second coffee date, the sun was out and there was no umbrella to force us to walk close together, but once again we bumped shoulders and elbows. Then suddenly the memory came back to me of my Spanish language teacher explaining to the class about different expectations of personal space, comparing Latin America with the northern US. I stopped apologizing for walking close. In the café, we sat in armchairs next to each other, but I purposely tried to lean in rather than away. I watched what Eduardo was doing and adapted my personal distance borders and facial expressions to reflect my best guess at what might make him feel comfortable. I learned why he had really moved to Auckland and about the stresses of finding housing and the challenges of his job.

For most of the coffee time, I felt a bit uncomfortable. I kept telling myself, "Don't pull away. Lean in." Sure, this was a second coffee date rather than a first, but it felt completely different to me. I was trying to tune in to Eduardo's expectations and behaviors, to create a comfortable, friendly atmosphere. Whether because of the sunshine, the latte, or my change in behavior, our second chat was definitely more open, honest, and personal.

When we interact in situations in which different rules of behavior may be in play, getting information in advance about how to show respect, how to be polite, and what the expectations are is both polite and wise. We should do our homework when we are the hosts but also when we are the guests. In either case, a cultural insider with experiences in both our culture and the other culture can provide valuable information and insights. In situations involving a mix of cultures, finding the best compromise can be challenging. The situation can feel strange for everyone if we try to change everything to model the guest culture. Plus, if we all try to dress differently or be someone we are not, we can trespass into appropriation (taking something from someone or someone's cultures without permission for our own selfish uses). **So while a list of do's and don'ts can be helpful, what we need to do most of all is follow the cycle for navigating cultural differences.** This process involves the following three steps and is portrayed in figure 5.1.

1. **Ask** help of insiders or persons with significant experiences in both cultures.
2. **Reflect** on what others are doing. What are appropriate ways to show respect? How could we adapt our behaviors, and which options seem best?
3. **Adapt** to the situation. Assume that everyone wants to be respectful, personable, and reasonable. Do our best to make others feel comfortable. Be patient with awkwardness or missteps and be willing to discuss these cultural mistakes if doing so isn't inappropriate. This step brings us back to the first one: ask others for help.

Figure 5.1. The Cycle for Navigating Cultural Differences

In planning for encounters with a mix of cultures we need to consider how common social values such as respect, kindness, hospitality, and politeness are acted out in different cultural contexts.

RECOGNIZING OUR CULTURAL BIASES

Understanding how specific behaviors link to social values differently in different cultures can help us get beyond a list of do's and don'ts as defined by *our* viewpoint. I teach German language and culture courses. Not so long ago, a Spanish-speaking colleague helped me see how my list of do's and don'ts and my ideas about etiquette were still completely on my terms, in other words, biased by my cultural perspectives. He explained, "You know, people say that Germans are always on time and that in my culture everyone is always late. But that isn't really true. In both cultures, things start on time. In your culture [German], 'on time' is the exact time written on the invitation and shown on the clock. In my culture, 'on time' is when everyone has arrived."

"To effectively communicate, we must realize that we are all different in the way we perceive the world and use this understanding as a guide to our communication with others."
—Tony Robbins

When I told this story recently, someone in the audience commented that the non-German way of being on time is so inconsiderate because it makes everyone wait for whomever is late. Of course, the flipside of that perspective might be that the German way of starting at a specific time on the clock without waiting for everyone to arrive is inconsiderate to the invited people and their right to be included.

Both of these comments helped me rethink how I talk to my students about punctuality. For example, what if I said something like this: "In Germany, everything starts on time, not like in some countries where things always start late." This way of describing this social rule implies a value judgment: "on time" is defined as a specified time on the clock, and Germany does it right, while others are messed up. Nowadays, I try not to use "on time" in a way that implies one culture is right and another culture is wrong. In fact, I usually get students to tell me what they think being on time means in their different contexts and situations. We discuss the ideas and values that different cultures have as demonstrated in how they think about being on time. Is it based on units of clock time and the value of minutes as a commodity? Or is time not quite so chopped up into planned and measured bits? A discussion of being on time is linked to the idea of cultural dimensions—how cultures think about broad issues. I still want my students to learn the social rules: when in Germany, they really ought to show up at the exact clock time. But I also want my students to see how this rule for behavior is linked to a system of practices, cultural dimensions, and guiding orientations or ways of living.

Being good hosts and guests, especially when an event will have a mix of cultures, involves doing our homework. We should learn about the likely expectations and social rules of the different groups, consider how to make everyone feel welcome, and try to anticipate areas of misunderstanding. Most importantly, we need to adjust our frame of reference; in other words, **we need to understand that our expectations and definitions of politeness, being on time, modesty, fairness, and many other things are not *the* definitions against which the behaviors of the entire world should be measured. By building ICQ skills, we are better able to discuss and navigate our different expectations** without anyone feeling as if their way of doing things is always being labeled as the wrong way.

TOURIST VERSUS SOJOURNER

My oldest child spent a semester in Hungary and told me how he figured out that he had somehow changed from a visitor to a local: "When the little old ladies poke you and tell you to lift their shopping roller bags onto the streetcar for them, you know you no longer look like a tourist in Budapest." This came after he had figured out the public transportation. He learned to automatically offer his seat to any person who looked older than his parents, and he mastered the phrases necessary to do so in Hungarian. Being usefully "local" began with building his knowledge, then following the rules, doing what locals did, and making an effort to learn how to communicate a little in the language. One of his culture course assignments was to make a location in Budapest one of *his* places: go there often, be a regular, become familiar, notice the other people and how the place changes with the daylight or the seasons. What a great assignment! He chose a hummus bar. Not only did he get to eat a lot of hummus, but he also developed a sense of place, a small toehold of belonging in a culture completely foreign to him. He got to practice observing and, in some ways, contributing to the community in that little corner restaurant in Budapest. One day he proudly reported that he was a regular after the server one evening asked him if he was going to order "the usual."

> *"Integral to the art of travel is the longing to break away from the stultifying habits of our lives at home, and to break away for however long it takes to once again truly see the world around us."*
> —Phil Cousineau

In the research and writing about studying or working abroad, one recurring theme is the goal to move beyond being a tourist toward becoming a sojourner. This distinction is similar to my son's experience of visitor versus local, although becoming a functioning local generally takes a longer stay—weeks, months, or even years. In contrast, the key differences between a tourist and a sojourner approach can help us in any intercultural situation, whether short or long term, whether far away or close to home. These terms can help us reflect on how we go about engaging across cultural lines and why. In short, what is our underlying strategy or approach? Some of the key differences between a tourist and a sojourner approach are summarized in Figure 5.2.

Figure 5.2. Comparing Tourist and Sojourner Approaches

Tourist	Sojourner
It's about having fun and being entertained.	It's about encountering and engaging.
There is a focus on transactions, exchanges, and acquisition.	There is a focus on relationships, understanding, and sharing.
I want to feel good.	I want to grow.
It's all about me.	It's all about us.

Popular travel writer Rick Steves tells a story about an encounter with a dervish, a type of Muslim monk. He was invited to observe the dervish's prayer ritual of spinning in a meditative dance but only if he learned what the different positions and movements meant spiritually. Steves concluded, "Watching a dervish whirl can be a cruise-ship entertainment option . . . or a spiritual awakening." His insight changed the way I talk to my students about "entertainments" across cultural lines. We can enjoy the food or the dance, the music or the festival, but we can also try to understand another way of seeing our world, of creating meaning in a community and in our lives.

While Steves writes travel books, his insight applies to how we engage with others across cultural lines and how we work together to build community at home. If we adopt a tourist approach to ICQ for community building, we will have a few feel-good moments and perhaps some fun. We will exchange stories and possibly create a space that is safe enough to have a conversation or two but that is nobody's home. A tourist approach creates an artificial neutral zone where we superficially work together briefly before retreating to our real living spaces.

In contrast, a sojourner approach to ICQ for community building builds relationships. The stories we tell one another are not just about exchanging anecdotes. We share pieces of ourselves in order to understand one another better. As we learn and understand more, our relationships become the foundation and support beams, the social capital for a strong community. We also need to move beyond doing this community building just so that we can feel less guilty or we can be understood better. **If we commit to sojourning together, we will each grow as we all grow together.** In the end, the project is focused on creating a new us—a community in which we all have a foothold, a secure position from which further progress can be made.

HOSPITALITY AND BELONGING

For each of us to have this foothold in our community, **we need to be a community that extends hospitality and understands the need for a sense of belonging.** Alison and David moved into apartment 2A at the same time that my husband and I moved into 1B. Our two apartments shared a wall. In that first month at some point almost every day, Alison would stop by to say hello. Sometimes she had a question, sometimes she brought cookies, sometimes she wanted to borrow the large stockpot. She would often stay a short while, chatting about the weather and her family back home in Australia. When she left, then I could get back to my work. At first, her visits were a little awkward, but after a while, they became normal. Over time, I realized that what she did for me was much more than offer a break from my university studies. She made it okay for me to just stop by and visit her in her apartment, to take some of her time to vent about a rotten day, or to borrow an egg. She gave me the opportunity to host her short visits, and as I did so, I learned how to be more hospitable. She taught me the value of creating space in my life to host, to listen to, and to provide for others. In short, she made that little neighborhood of student apartments into a welcoming community.

Hospitality at a basic level is noticing people in our spaces or in common spaces and sharing what we have (cookies, stockpots, or stories). At a deeper level, hospitality is welcoming others and recognizing their right to belong. Hospitality involves making others feel welcome, learning together, building the community that now also includes Us & Them. It involves listening to their stories, which, like a positive cycle of good, helps them feel like they have a voice in this new community; their experiences and perspectives contribute value to the whole.

So how does ICQ connect to hospitality and community building? We need ICQ skills to know how to make others feel welcome, how to show respect and be polite. Building our ICQ involves building our knowledge, our interpretation skills, and our interpersonal skills in order to be good guests but also to be better hosts. Whether we are outside our comfort zones or hosting others in our spaces, we need to learn how to interpret actions and reactions, especially when they are not exactly what we would do. We need to have some shared tools and common vocabulary so that when there are misunderstandings, we have a better chance of asking good questions and figuring out what is going on. And we need to recognize our own biases, perspectives, and identities so that we can better observe and understand the same in others. The others we engage with should feel that we are trying to understand who they are and what we can learn from them, not that we view and define them based solely on *our* operating definitions.

Contemporary philosopher and theologian Miroslav Volf has written a great deal on issues related to cross-cultural understanding. In his book *Exclusion and Embrace*, he uses the metaphor of embrace to describe how to relate to others. When we hear "embrace," we might think of hugging those we love or of greeting others, and we probably associate embrace with the idea of approving of something or adopting something (as in, "The committee embraced the new plan."). **Volf's metaphor of embrace, however, is not about adopting or acquiring something or someone into ourselves.**

> *"There is no hospitality like understanding."*
> —Vanna Bonta

Rather, we open our arms to invite someone into an embrace. This is like extending hospitality and recognizing the right of others to belong. **Embrace means listening to the stories and experiences of others and trying to understand them from their perspectives, allowing others a space in the community, and seeing or saying yes to a vision of those others together with us in community.** When the embrace is over, we might go back to our original shape. They do not become just like us, and we do not mysteriously become some type of hybrid. But embrace changes us. Why? Because in that act of welcoming another and being welcomed by another, we changed our shape to make space. For a brief time, we tuned our hearts to listen to and understand a story other than our own. That experience becomes part of our individual memory and our group experience.

The ICQ skills support community building because ICQ skills help us be better hosts and guests and enable us to create a sense of belonging. **Communities are strongest when the members feel they are welcome, understood, and truly belong.**

BRIDGES AND PATHWAYS

Great communities share a sense of commonness, of belonging, or of purpose. Nothing makes all the kids in a class bond together faster than when a new mean substitute teacher enters the picture. A common enemy makes fast friends. At times, community spirit is forged when something bad happens: a tragedy brings a town together to mourn and commemorate. A sense of community can be strong for positive reasons as well, such as when members of a community join together to root for the hometown team in a national tournament. Sometimes a community is created or strengthened because people are working together toward a common goal, such as when another car accident gets all the neighbors to petition for a stoplight at a nearby intersection.

As we all build our own ICQ, we are also working on common goals. We are learning more about ICQ and how it can help us. First, at a personal level, ICQ helps us understand what makes us who we are: the cultural dimensions of our broad cultures; the products, practices, and perspectives that are part of our everyday lives; the guiding orientations of our subcultures and microcultures; the stereotypes or biases we carry with us; our experiences and stories. We have a chance to step back and consider which pieces of our identities are core, negotiable, or additional. We can explore each of these things also at the level of our local communities. Whether we are trying to improve or create good community in the workplace, the school, the volunteer team, or the neighborhood, understanding who we are as a community and what we hope to be is part of our journey together.

Critical to this project is that we have to want to be on this journey and to build relationships across cultural lines. This goes beyond throwing some time and resources toward "bridge building" and then leaving it unused like a bridge to nowhere. In fact, perhaps we shouldn't think about building a bridge but rather creating a path. When I toured The Hobbit movie set in New Zealand, I learned all sorts of fun trivia, including the immense amount of work that went into making things look old, like purposely soaking wooden beams in chemicals and distressing them, painting and scraping and painting them again. There were no two-hundred-year-old hobbit holes, so they made new ones that looked old. Near Bagshot Row (the grassy line of doors where the main character Bilbo lives), our guide, Simon, stood beside one of the hobbit holes. "See the clothesline up there?" He pointed to the hill atop the hobbit home. We all looked at the humble, child-sized shirt hung with wooden pins on a string between two rough poles. "Peter Jackson made one of the staff hang up and take down that shirt every day the set was under construction and the filming was happening. Why?" One of the kids on the tour piped up: "So the path would look real." Simon smiled. "So the path would *be* real." Although Jackson had to artificially create two-hundred-year-old hobbit homes, he could authentically create a well-worn path in the grass by this one hobbit hole, and he did.

ICQ for community building isn't about building a nice-looking bridge, admiring our work, and then returning to our previous lives. Rather, in time together and with emerging ICQ skills, we can begin creating paths across lines of difference—paths that will become more visible and usable as we meet along them—and relationships that look genuine because they are. Sometimes this work can be tedious; sometimes we will have twenty other things that seem more important. **But for this divisive, polarized time, we need to roll up our sleeves and figure out how to find something we can like about one another, look for things we can agree on, and increase our capacity for understanding people and ideas different from our own. We need to have some good conversations and relationships with people who aren't always on the same side of every issue as we are.** As a society or community, we cannot hope to have strong networks of genuine relationships across cultural lines unless we make a point to create paths and meet along them again and again and again.

SEEING DIFFERENCE DIFFERENTLY

Differences do not always have to divide us. Seeing others as part of "us" is critical at every level of society: families, neighborhoods, communities, you name it. In 1974, First Lady Betty Ford shocked the nation by making very public her battle with breast cancer. Breast cancer was a disease affecting part of the body that for women was literally and figuratively kept under wraps; breast cancer was talked about only in intimate circles; and, generally, getting this diagnosis marked you as "sick" and an "outsider." When Mrs. Ford came out about her breast cancer, she changed all that. Newscasters found themselves saying the word "breast" on the air. Breast cancer was something our beloved First Lady was dealing with. She was, after all, one of us, and that shifted how we thought about other people with breast cancer. Suddenly, people with breast cancer were part of the insider group.

Differences can make us stronger. My favorite types of family games are the cooperative ones. This is especially true since one of my children has become an incredible strategist and wins competitive games far too often for his own good. When playing our favorite cooperative games, having someone who is good at the details; someone who can always see the big picture; someone who likes keeping all the tokens, cards, and little gems organized; and someone who has just baked chocolate chip cookies really helps. You get the idea: our community can become richer, have a greater variety of skills to put to use, and accomplish great things by using our diversity to our advantage.

Differences are opportunities. Imagine you love books and libraries. Perhaps you have visited your local library so many times that you have lost count. Free books. What could be better? Then imagine that one day you learn that there is actually a basement and an attic in this library filled with thousands of books that were not in the catalog. These volumes are now available to the public. Woo-hoo! Getting to know cultures, peoples, and ideas different from our own can be like that: new foods, new songs, new ideas, new approaches to old problems. And we can each share our favorite things with others.

> "Diversity may be the hardest thing for a society to live with, and perhaps the most dangerous thing for a society to be without."
> —William Sloan Coffin Jr

When we begin to understand the thinking and feelings, the stories and experiences of others, their way of doing and being in the world, then we start to see those "different" people as three dimensional human beings. Differences do not have to be a problem to be solved; differences can be a learning opportunitunity and something to be embraced. Seeing differences as something potentially positive for all of us can motivate us to make time for one another, to share experiences, to walk in each other's shoes, to partner for good causes. That is when our relationships become real and not token, and that is how our communities grow strong.

MORE THAN GOOD INTENTIONS

Our best intentions and a genuine desire for connections with others are absolutely necessary for this project of improving communities by building relationships that cross the traditional or de facto divisions. But goodwill alone is not enough. Years ago, I was flying from Michigan to Florida and had a conversation with the stranger next to me. At the end of nearly two hours, he smiled and said, "You know, your English is almost perfect." You can hypothesize about why he said this by pulling up ideas from chapters 1–3. Maybe his stereotypes of Asian people made him unable to hear my English as normal. Perhaps in his experiences people who look like me did not grow up speaking English, and so based on that, I probably didn't either. Perhaps he was an English teacher and my use of "who" instead of "whom" added to his stereotypes so that he somehow labeled me as a nonnative English speaker. Maybe he just didn't know that millions of people in the Midwest of the US sound just like I do and that English is indeed their first, native, and maybe only language. I know he was trying to pay me a compliment; his intentions were good. But he was missing some Cultural Intelligence about Asians, about American English dialects, and about his own stereotypes and biases. His well-meaning comment became an insult.

One of the roadblocks to building relationships across cultural lines is that our many differences can make us uncomfortable around one another. We need to practice engaging across lines of difference. The more I understand about myself and cultural differences, the better I can interpret what is causing us or me to feel uncomfortable. The more we learn from one another about one another, the stronger our relationships can become. The more we do these things, the less strange they feel. When my youngest, whose school clothes of choice generally consisted of sweat pants and T-shirts, moved to a new country and a new school, he suddenly had to wear a strictly enforced school uniform, including a collared shirt tucked into dressy shorts or trousers secured with a black leather belt. He resigned himself to this fate and complained only every other day for the first two weeks. But one Saturday about a month in, he meandered into the kitchen in search of breakfast and said casually, "You know, it feels sort of strange not to tuck my shirt in." Practice does not necessarily make perfect, but it can make something feel less strange.

The added bonus of an ICQ approach to getting to know others is that we also learn a great deal about ourselves. This learning is not always easy as we make space in our hearts and minds for other people. **Building our ICQ does not eliminate the risks or the discomfort that crossing cultural lines might involve, but ICQ helps reframe the possible consequences and benefits of engaging with others.**

- I am not risking my sense of identity; I am exposing myself to the possibility of becoming more than I am alone.
- I am not muddying my faith or perspectives on life; I am sharpening my understanding of what I believe by considering other ways of seeing the world.
- I am not losing who I am; I am using who I am to help us all learn from one another.

QUESTIONS TO CONSIDER

1. Which products or practices make you feel comfortable when you are invited into a new situation, such as a new job or department at work, a new worshiping community, a new school, or a new club or group?

2. What do you think are the biggest roadblocks that might prevent you from building relationships across cultural lines?

NOTES AND RESOURCES

Quotations in this chapter are taken from Anthony Robbins, *Unlimited Power. The New Science of Personal Achievement* (New York: Free Press, 1997), 237; Phil Cousineau, *The Art of Pilgrimage: The Seeker's Guide to Making Travel Sacred* (New York: MJF Books, 1998), 23; Vanna Bonta, *Flight: A Quantum Fiction Novel* (New York: Meridian Publishing, 1996), chapter 48; and William Sloan Coffin, Jr. *The Heart is a Little to the Left* (New Hampshire: Dartmouth College Press, 2011), 70.

83 **eleventh juror:** Reginald Rose, *Twelve Angry Men* (New York: Penguin Classics, 2005), 59.

87 **Tourist versus Sojourner:** This way of thinking about travel and studying abroad, sometimes distinguished by the terms *tourist* versus *pilgrim*, is referred to in numerous books, such as Ronald J. Morgan and Cynthia Toms Smedley, eds., *Transformations at the Edge of the World: Forming Global Christians through the Study Abroad Experience* (Abilene, TX: Abilene Christian University Press, 2010); Susan Cahill, *The Smiles of Rome: A Literary Companion for Readers and Travelers* (New York: Ballatine Books, 2005), and Donald De Graaf, *There and Back: Living and Learning Abroad* (Grand Rapids, MI: Calvin College Press, 2015).

89 **Popular travel writer Rick Steves:** See Rick Steves, *Travel as a Political Act, 3rd* edition (Edmond, WA: Rick Steves, 2018).

89 **Hospitality and Belonging:** These are common values in cultures throughout the world. The history of hospitality is summarized in Kevin O'Gorman, *The Origins of Hospitality and Tourism* (Oxford: Goodfellow Publishers, 2010). A brief reflection on issues of hospitality and belonging from a Christian perspective can be found in David I. Smith and Pennylyn Dykstra-Pruim, *Christians and Cultural Difference* (Grand Rapids, MI: Calvin College Press, 2016). Miroslav Volf's book *Exclusion and Embrace* (Nashville, TN: Abingdon Press, 1996), though challenging, is foundational reading for learners interested in reconciliation across cultural lines.

91 **Contemporary philosopher and theologian:** Miroslav Volf, *Exclusion and Embrace, Revised and Updated: A Theological Exploration of Identity, Otherness, and Reconciliation* (Nashville, TN: Abingdon Press, 2019).

95 **your English is almost perfect:** The comment about my English being almost perfect is a type of microaggression. This term is defined and explored in chapter 2's learning kit activity 2D.

96 **I am not losing who I am; I am using who I am:** "Don't lose who you are. Use who you are" was used as a slogan in an ad compaign (2015) to promote joining the New Zealand police force. This ad seemed to target persons of color and highlighted an officer of Maori heritage.

Book Suggestion

Yang Liu, *East Meets West* (Mainz, Germany: Hermann Schmidt Mainz, 2010) is a book that contains Liu's infographic artistic representations of key cultural differences between her two cultures: Japanese and German. Originally part of an art exhibition, her stark, poignant, and often humorous images are also available online by googling "Yang Liu images," accessed October 31, 2018. They highlight such differences as orientation toward time, rules for waiting in line, and ideas of beauty.

Film Suggestions

The Namesake (2006) PG-13. American-born Gogol struggles with his Indian heritage, his traditional parents, and his US-American cultures. The film portrays his family history, his parents' story, and his journey back and forth between cultural identities.

Zootopia (2016) PG. "In a city of anthropomorphic animals, a rookie bunny cop and a cynical con-artist fox must work together to uncover a conspiracy" (IMDb). In this family-friendly animated film, cultures clash, stereotypes get in the way, and intercultural cooperation is necessary to save the day.

Conclusion

You may be lucky to have an ICQ group in which the short-term relationships become long-term ones. But even if this is not the case, you have hopefully begun a lifelong journey of ICQ building that equips you to nurture stronger relationships across lines of difference. This is not an easy road, but it is something we desperately need in our cities and country. Right now. The fabric of our nation has holes, some might say chasms or walls, that divide us. Choose your favorite metaphor. There are pockets of strength and resources, of skills and stories, but we are held together by far too few strands of friendship. Diversity initiatives may be changing the mix in some of our organizations, but to realize inclusion and to reap the real benefits of that diversity, we need Interpersonal Cultural Intelligence.

The same knowledge, interpretation, and interpersonal skills that can help corporate executives locally and nationally are desperately needed by all of us at many levels: in worshiping congregations, schools, neighborhood associations, political committees, and of course the international arena as well. With airline travel, smartphones, and the internet, our world is more connected than ever, but in some ways, these are bridges created by technology and not the paths worn through personal relationships. We need to build relationships across cultural lines, and goodwill alone is not enough. **We need to improve our Interpersonal Cultural Intelligence (ICQ) skills so that our efforts are effective, our goodwill is understood as such, and we can see, anticipate, interpret, and navigate in better ways the differences that are dividing our communities, country, and world.**

Introduction to the ICQ
Group Learning Kits

Each chapter has a corresponding learning kit for ICQ groups to use together. The book is designed so that a group of people commit to reading the chapters on their own, perhaps one chapter per week. Then the group meets, again perhaps once per week, to discuss and reflect on what members are learning about Interpersonal Cultural Intelligence and community building. The learning kits provide learning activities and story sharing or conversation prompts that help members reflect together on the main points of each chapter and build ICQ skills through practice during the meeting times.

Some of the activities are more analytical, while some are more feelings-oriented. Some are introvert-friendly, and some will appeal more to extroverted types. Some activities may be more appropriate for certain groups than for others. The ICQ for community building facilitators should choose which activities might be most beneficial for their specific group and goals and what if any adjustments to the activities would be appropriate.

Each learning kit contains the following:

- chapter summary
- two questions to help you recall main points
- learning activities and story sharing prompts
- next steps
- an "I can . . ." self-assessment for key points of that chapter

Learning Kit 1
for Chapter 1

What Is Interpersonal Cultural Intelligence for Community Building?

CHAPTER 1 SUMMARY

Interpersonal Cultural Intelligence (ICQ) is the capacity to engage in constructive ways with people who are different from us and with ideas that are different from our own using an understanding of cultures and cultural identities.

ICQ can help us build relationships across cultural lines in effective, gracious, and positive ways.

We can all improve our ICQ over time by focusing on three skill areas:

- knowledge about cultural identities
- interpretation of practices and perspectives
- interpersonal skills for interaction and dialogue with others

The ICQ for community building project encourages groups of people to learn about cultural identities, learn together, and share stories in order to understand others and themselves better. Improving our ICQ builds our capacity to react to and interact with other people and perspectives in more informed ways.

RECALLING CHAPTER 1

1. What did you learn or wonder about after taking the ICQ self-survey?

2. What got you interested in participating in an ICQ for community building book group? What are you hoping for?

1A. BUILDING ICQ THROUGH INTRODUCTIONS

BEYOND SMALL TALK

Usually in group settings, people make small talk about jobs or kids or the weather, but in this activity, you want to start building relationships and inviting stories. We are going to practice getting to know another person almost by conducting a type of research.

You can ask about	in order to . . .
facts and fun things	get to know about the person
habits and goals	think about what they might enjoy or what would make them feel welcome
perspectives, beliefs, or values	understand how they see the world and why

Read through the questions in the table below. If any seem inappropriate or sensitive for your group, do not use those questions. Pair up with someone you do not already know well. Using at least some of the questions below, get to know each other a little. After working in pairs, take the opportunity to share some of the interesting things you learned about each other with the whole group.

facts and fun things (knowledge)	• What is one of your favorite foods and why? Is there a memory or family tradition that is connected to this food? • What three objects would you bring in for show and tell to introduce yourself to others? • Name something you have done that surprised people or surprised yourself. Why was it surprising or unexpected? What made it interesting for you?
habits and goals (behaviors)	• When you have free time, what do you enjoy doing most? What makes this activity particularly enjoyable for you? • What is something in your life that you are proud of or happy about? What about that event or thing makes it special for you? • If you could wave a magic wand and change one thing about your life right now, what would it be?
perspectives, beliefs, or values (interpretation and motivations)	• What three things do you hope people will say about you or remember about you when you are no longer alive? • If you could custom order a best friend, what would he or she be like? • Think of someone who is a hero or role model for you. What about this person do you admire?

Practice having relationship-building conversations. You can use some of these questions to express interest in getting to know others beyond a superficial level or for inviting a deeper conversation with your grandfather or your daughter. You can also think about the types of things that you can share easily about yourself so that others can feel you are opening up to them.

PERSONALITIES
PREFERENCES
GROUP DYNAMICS

1B. GETTING TO KNOW YOURSELF AND OTHERS

Step 1: Place your pencil in the very center of the grid below. In response to each pair of words at the bottom of the page, move your pencil one line to the left or to the right based on which word describes you better. Don't think about the words too long or too hard. Go with your gut reaction. Mark where you end up on the thick horizontal line.

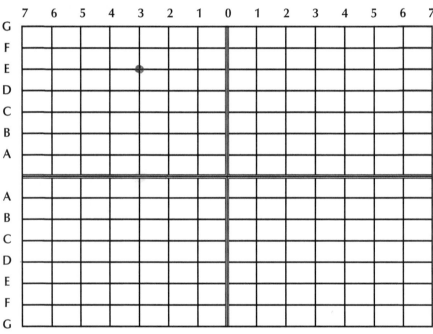

Step 1:

← LEFT	RIGHT →
← informal	formal →
← subjective	objective →
← accommodating	competitive →
← harmonious	correct →
← relationship-oriented	task-oriented →
← considerate	analytical →
← caring	strong-minded →

Step 2:

↑ LEFT	RIGHT ↓
↑ quiet	talkative ↓
↑ observant	involved ↓
↑ inward-focused	outward-focused ↓
↑ reserved	flamboyant ↓
↑ reflective	action-oriented ↓
↑ thoughtful	outspoken ↓
↑ cautious	bold ↓

Step 2: Rotate this page so that you can read the text under "Step 2" on the previous page. Place your pencil where you last were on the grid. With the book in a landscape orientation, move your pencil left or right in response to this new set of words based on which one describes you better.

Step 3: Mark the spot on the grid where you landed at the end of step 2. What does this landing spot mean? Each quadrant represents a set of personality tendencies according to one way of analyzing personalities. (There are many different systems for doing this.) If you hold the page in the portrait orientation again, here is the very simple summary:

earthy green feelers and introverts	cool blue thinkers and introverts
sunshine yellow feelers and extroverts	fiery red thinkers and extroverts

If you are a very visual person, coloring in the quandrants might help in processing and remembering take-aways from this activity.

Step 4: Share your results with the others by telling them your quadrant and your landing spot on the grid. For example, "I am a sunshine yellow. My landing point was F2." You can get a sense for the entire group by placing dots on a master grid for all to see.

What does this mean? This simplified personality indicator helps you see where you might be on two personality factors: introvert versus extrovert and thinker versus feeler. This activity can be used to spark your awareness and begin a conversation. What can you gain?

- It is a way to begin thinking about what you do and like and why. Why do you hate group work and love a good lecture, while others find those same things boring or intimidating?
- This helps you get a first feel for the different personalities in the room and the strengths or talents that each person can contribute.
- In all likelihood, you will feel most comfortable working with people most like you. Feeling welcome is important, but being comfortable all the time is not a top priority for the ICQ community building project.

- You should consider how you need the strengths of the others in the group. A fiery red might make a good discussion leader, but they need the earthy greens to remember to think about people's feelings. A cool blue might provide good analysis for a problem that is a great foundation for the enthusiastic sunshine yellows. Be aware of how different people like to work and work best in these group settings and try to help one another as much as possible.

Your quadrant should not become a permanent label for you or your neighbor. Your responses can vary depending on the context you are imagining. For example, you might be a much more talkative person when you are with the office staff and much quieter when you are in a Bible study group. You might also find that you change over time.

Questions for the Group

Which color or quadrant has the most people? Which has the fewest?

earthy green: feelers and introverts	cool blue: thinkers and introverts
sunshine yellow: feelers and extroverts	fiery red: thinkers and extroverts

How many people ended up close to the center (ABC and 123) on the original grid?

How many people ended up farther from the center (EFG and 567) on the original grid?

Are the majority of people close to the center (ABC and 123) or farther from the center (EFG and 567)? If many group members ended up farther from the center, the personality differences within the group might seem starker.

Based on the information above, answer these questions:

- What might be one of the strengths of this group?
- What important perspectives or approaches are less dominant but need to be acknowledged and remembered?

1C. AGREEING ON GROUND RULES

In this activity, you work together to come up with a few community ground rules for conversation.

Drafting community ground rules

As you work your way through *Understanding Us & Them*, you will get to use several tools to help explore and understand cultural differences. As a community of learners, you will also develop some common vocabulary to have deeper, richer conversations about and across lines of difference. For all this work together, we want to create a brave space.

A brave space is where each person can participate or be brave because there is no fear of insult, injury, or aggression. We can still engage in hot topics or deep conversations but we do so with a generous curiosity toward other people, their opinions, and their stories.

Consider some of the following possible ground rules for community conversations. Which would you like to adopt for this book club community? Which would you like to change or rewrite and how? What rules do you think are missing? Small groups can draft their own short list of ground rules and then share them with the whole group.

Examples of community ground rules for conversation are offered below, with thanks to various groups I have worked with.

Confidentiality
- **Maintain confidentiality**. What is said, stays. Names and specific details of shared stories will stay confidential (stay in the room) unless you specifically ask the person if his, her, or their story and name(s) may be shared outside the group.
- **What is learned can be shared.** Ideas, new ways of thinking, keen insights can be shared outside the group without specifically identifying individuals from the group.

Listening to learn
- **Be open to new perspectives.** Don't pre-judge or make assumptions about others' experiences or identities.
- **Listen in order to learn from others and their stories.** Listening to someone's story or perspective is not an exercise in preparing for how to debate about their experience, discount their reaction, or win the next argument.

- **Sharing a personal story is optional.** A person can opt to "pass."

Respect, Caring, and Charity

- **Respect others' experiences, perspectives and emotions.** When we respond to someone's story, we will try to be affirming not negative, disbelieving, or derogatory.
- **Be caring toward others.** We all make mistakes. We may have been shaped by mis-information. We all have biases or blind spots.
- **Value relationships over winning, being clever, or appearing smart.**
- **Respect different levels of emotions or expression of emotions.** Some folks are expressive, while some are reserved. Some view emotional expressions as a sign of positive vulnerability, while emotional sharing can make others feel uncomfortable.

Responding to others' stories

- **Sometimes silence is okay.**
- **Be honest in order to learn about ourselves and others.** It is okay to respond honestly to someone's story with how you feel, but that response should not be aggressive. Example responses: That makes me feel sad/angry/confused/ encouraged/hopeful.

THREE SKILL AREAS OF INTERPERSONAL CULTURAL INTELLIGENCE

1D. REVIEWING THE ICQ SKILLS

Review the key ICQ skills by filling in the blanks in the graphic below.

KNOWLEDGE about cultural _____

INTERPRETATION of _____ and _____

INTERPERSONAL SKILLS for _____ and _____

The three statements below are taken from the self-survey in chapter 1. Discuss the following with a partner: Which ICQ skill area does each statement relate to: knowledge, interpretation, or interpersonal skills?

- I can explain how my personal values influence my actions and reactions in different situations.
- I can explain how some of the things I do or the way I do things is linked to my ways of seeing the world.
- I can easily adjust my behaviors based on observations of others' interactions:
  - verbal behaviors (tone, volume, use of silence, rate of speaking)
  - nonverbal behaviors (eye contact, physical proximity, clothing choices, facial expressiveness, hand gestures)

Starting to build your ICQ skills

Knowledge: How would you describe your own cultural identity? (Consider what 5 – 7 words you would associate with your cultural identity.)

Interpretation: Give some examples of something you do regularly that is linked to what you think is important in life. (Which habits or practices are particularly important in your life?)

Interpersonal skills: Give an example of adjusting how you communicate or interact because you believe another person would appreciate it.

1E. WARMING UP TO STORY SHARING

These sets of speaking prompts are springboards for each person to begin telling a bit about themselves. Divide into small groups of 3-4 persons. Decide which set of prompts or topics you wish to focus on, or allow the people in your group to choose freely. Some group members might be most comfortable if they are told in advance to prepare for this activity.

"The shortest distance between two people is a story."
—Patty Digh

SHARING ABOUT YOURSELF

Speaking prompts set 1 – Personality types (if you skipped activity 1B then skip this set of prompts and proceed to set 2, 3, or 4 below):

My results from activity 1B suggest that I am a . . .

} __ strong
__ moderate
__ borderline

} __ fiery red
__ earthy green
__ sunshine yellow
__ cool blue

This surprised (did not surprise) me because . . .

Speaking prompts set 2 - Feeling comfortable in a group:

I feel most comfortable in a group setting when . . .

I can feel uncomfortable in a group setting when . . .

I could probably feel comfortable sharing some of my stories with this group if . . .

Speaking prompts set 3 – Why I joined this ICQ group:

I became interested in joining this ICQ for community building project because . . .

I am interested in learning more about crossing cultural lines because . . .

Understanding Us & Them *seems like a good book group idea because ...*

Speaking prompts set 4 – Thinking about lines of difference:

I have noticed lines of difference in my communities or my life. For example, . . .

When I think about engaging across lines of difference, I feel ...

If I had to describe my recent experiences engaging with cultures or ideas different from my own, I would say ...

1F. STORY SHARING: REFLECTIONS ON COMMUNITY

This activity helps you begin sharing your dreams and hopes for community building.

Step 1: Working in a small group of 3-4 persons, start the conversation about what your ideal community looks like. Here are a few story sharing prompts to help you begin. Consider collecting responses from 1F to inform 1G.

I would love to	live	in a community that . . .
	work	
	worship	
	go to school	
	_____	

If I had to choose three words to describe the community I dream of living in, they would be . . .

One story I know of how a community came together is . . .

I think that a good community is most important when . . .

In my experience, some key factors in strong communities are . . .

One of the best community experiences I have had is . . .

Step 2: Discuss together some positive characteristics of the communities you live in and also some things that could change for the better. One way to focus your conversation and prepare to report back to the whole group is to complete these two sentences: "I like …." and "What if …."

I like . . .	What if . . .

1G. DRAFTING VISION AND MISSION STATEMENTS

WHAT ARE WE ALL ABOUT?

What is your ICQ book group all about? This activity is a chance to work out the answer together.

Warm-up

Many organizations develop statements about who they are and what they do. Below are mission statements for some well-known companies. Can you guess which company goes with each statement?

Mission Statement	Organization or Company
A. To connect people with their world, everywhere they live and work, and do it better than anyone else.	
B. To help customers improve and maintain their biggest asset—their home.	
C. To organize the world's information and make it universally accessible and useful.	
D. To be the world's favorite for American Style.	
E. To give people the power to share and make the world more open and connected.	
F. To make the world a more caring place by helping people laugh, love, heal, say thanks, reach out, and make meaningful connections with others.	
G. To inspire and nurture the human spirit—one person, one cup, and one neighborhood at a time.	

Answers are located below.

About Mission and Vision Statements

A **mission statement** concentrates on the present; it defines the core purpose, the people involved, and the reasons why something is important. What should be accomplished?

Answers to Warm-up
A. AT&T   B. Lowe's   C. Google   D. Gap, Inc.
E. Facebook   F. Hallmark   G. Starbucks

A **vision statement** focuses on the future; it is a source of inspiration and motivation. Often, it describes not just the future of the organization but also the future of the industry or the society in which the organization hopes to effect change. What effects do we hope to realize? What should be pursued?

The purpose of this activity is to bring focus and consensus to the work of your group. Try writing a mission statement and a vision statement for your ICQ for community building team.

Option 1: Work in small groups of 3-4 persons. Each small group can present their idea for a mission statement and/or a vision statement to the large group.

Option 2: Work as a whole group to determine key phrases or elements of a mission and/or a vision statement.

These statements should be fairly brief, and exact wording does not need to be stressed. Summaries of the group conversations from 1E and 1F can be integrated. The questions below can also help you draft your statements.

Mission Statement	Vision Statement
What do we do?	What are our hopes and dreams?
How do we do it?	What problem are we solving for the greater good?
Whom do we do it for?	
What value are we bringing?	What outcomes or results will describe success?

Send or post these statements after the group meeting. If a consensus cannot be reached, post two variations of a mission statement and/or two variations of a vision statement on the wall at the beginning of the next meeting. Each person can vote for the one they prefer by placing a sticker dot on it.

NEXT STEPS

As you read and work through *Understanding Us & Them*, you will focus on key concepts for understanding how people and cultures are different and on skill building to engage in good ways across lines of difference. You will also have opportunities to ponder some big overarching questions for improving the communities we live in. Here are a few questions to start considering:

- What would be most important in my ideal community?
- How can we build community in the best ways possible given our circumstances?
- Who has to buy into this project?
- Which topics, issues, or concerns are likely to pose difficulties?
- What can I and my ICQ group do to improve our communities?

"I CAN . . ." SELF-CHECK FOR CHAPTER 1

For each "I can" statement, indicate how much you agree with it by circling yes or no or by marking a spot along the yes-no line in the right column.

I can tell someone what ICQ stands for.	Yes ---------------------- No
I can describe the purpose or cornerstones of ICQ for community building so that others have a reasonable idea what it is about.	Yes ---------------------- No
I can name the three skill areas of ICQ.	Yes ---------------------- No
I can describe why sharing stories is valuable for the ICQ for community building project.	Yes ---------------------- No
I can give an example of how different personalities or differences can be valuable to a community.	Yes ---------------------- No

Notes

The quotation in Learning Kit 1 is taken from Patty Digh, "Grant specificity to the other," filmed November 2017 in Indianapolis, IN, TEDx video 11:34, https://www.youtube.com/watch?v=3hVReRJCTHU

Activity 1B: This activity is an adaptation of a get-to-know-you activity led by Robert Nordling at a music camp for high school and university students.

Learning Kit 2
for Chapter 2

I and We—ICQ Knowledge

CHAPTER 2 SUMMARY

We are cultural beings.

- Cultural identities are complicated.
- We are a product of the cultures in which we were raised or feel at home.
- We see things as right or normal or logical against the backdrop of our specific cultures.
- Key pieces of our identities are shaped by our cultures.

We have to work at recognizing how powerful and destructive biases and stereotypes can be.

- Stereotypes are real. We all have them.
- A stereotype is not the whole picture or a realistic representation for an entire group.
- By learning and being open to new experiences, we can work past our stereotypes.
- When we get to know others and consider their perspectives, we can begin to change how we think, act, and feel toward them.

A culture is a system of products, practices, and perspectives that generally characterize a group.

RECALLING CHAPTER 2

1. Explain one example of a linked product, practice, and perspective. Your example could be from the chapter or from your own life and experiences.

2. What is an example of a stereotype that others may have of you or a group you belong to? How does that stereotype affect you and your everyday life?

CORE VALUES

2A. UNDERSTANDING YOUR OWN CULTURES

Think briefly about what is important to you in your cultures or subcultures. The box below contains some of the things that different cultures value and that they sometimes value differently.

group harmony	freedom	equality	family security
traditions	self-reliance	reputation	openness
privacy	spirituality	relationships	productivity

On your own

Each person takes a few minutes to fill in the table below. Which of the values in the box above are most important for the culture of the country in which you live? List at least five in the left column below, #1 being the most important in your opinion. Which of the values in the box above are the fundamental core values or beliefs for yourself and your family? List five and rank them in the right column.

	Core values for the country in which I live	Core values for myself/my family
#1		
#2		
#3		
#4		
#5		

Questions to consider

How do your personal values match up to the values of the country in which you live? Which of the statements below best fits the analysis of your right and left columns, of the values of the country in which you live and of you personally.

- I personally have very similar values to those of the country in which I live.
- I have some similar values and some different values compared to those of the country in which I live.
- I have very different values from those of the country in which I live.

When the country values and personal values align well, you are like a fish living in water: you might not think much about the culture in which you live. When there are many mismatches, you can feel like a fish out of water.

Were there other values or priorities that you wish had been in the original list? Is there a core value that you feel is really #1 for either the country in which you live or for you personally that was not in the box at the beginning of this activity?

Work with a partner

Partner task 1: Compare your rankings in the table above with a partner. How do the country lists (the left column for each of you) compare? How do the personal lists (the right column for each of you) compare?

Partner task 2: Look again at the list of values at the beginning of this exercise. Which one or two do you believe are *least* valued in your country and in your family? Fill in the table below for yourself and then compare with your partner.

	Least important values for the country in which I live	Least important values for myself/my family
#1		
#2		

Partner task 3: Analyze your core values lists. Compare the least important values you wrote above to the top two most important values previously. Do you and your partner agree about the values that are most and least valued in the country in which you live?

Do your least important values in your country and in your family harmonize, or are they at odds with each other?

How does looking at our perceptions of the core values of country and family help us think about our cultural identities?

2B. STORY SHARING: A PIECE OF YOUR STORY

Discussing some of the awkward or uncomfortable intercultural situations you have been in can help you and others reflect on how best to engage across lines of difference. You might have relevant experiences from traveling to a different country, city, or state; from changing schools or jobs; from going with a new friend to visit family or worship; from joining a new club or starting a new hobby; or, from volunteering or working with a new group of people. Break into small groups and discuss these situations using the following story sharing prompts:

A fish doesn't know he lives in water until he's hauled up on land.
- family saying

Sidebar: LEARNING FROM AWKWARD EXPERIENCES

- When have you felt "hauled up on land"?
- Was there a time when you felt out of place or uncomfortable because you didn't know what to do?
- What facts or information (knowledge about cultures or cultural identitites) would have helped you navigate that experience?

Here are some possible responses to use when listening to people's stories.

- How did that make you feel?
- How do you think the other person(s) felt?
- What do you wish you had done or said differently?
- What do you wish the other persons had done or asked you?
- Who would be a good person to ask for an insider perspective?
- Do you think that is a story you should or could share with the whole team?

What insights about engaging across cultural lines and the role of ICQ knowledge (information about cultures and cultural identities) came out of the stories in your small group? Collect these insights to share with the entire ICQ team.

2C. CONFRONTING STEREOTYPES

HOW WE SEE OTHERS

This activity can be done in small groups or as a whole ICQ team. #1 below can be done by each individual. #2 and #3 make for good group discussions.

1. Admit it. You've got 'em: stereotypes of others. Choose one group (culture or subculture) that you are interested in visiting, working with, or understanding better. On a piece of paper, electronic device, or in your mind, write down the clichés or stereotypes associated with that culture. You do not have to share these with anyone, so go ahead and be honest. After one minute of writing, scrunch up or shred the paper, delete the data, or imagine throwing it away.

2. Ask good questions. You want 'em: knowledge and facts to gain a better understanding of the group you just considered. Make a list of at least five questions you would like to ask an expert or a cultural insider. Come up with questions that could help you better understand the stereotypes you just threw away. Can others in the group either answer your questions or suggest where to find a good answer or whom to ask?

3. Recognize stereotypes around you. They've got 'em too: stereotypes of you. Make a list of ways in which you feel you have been stereotyped by others, perhaps because of your height, age, job status, ethnic background, accent, religious affiliation, clothing, education, or your brother Vinny. Who are these "others?" What do you think their stereotypes of you are based on? These can be written on sticky notes and posted on a board or shared with others. Take another few minutes to think beyond your national border. What stereotypes do others in the world often have of the people in your country or of your country as a whole? What do you think is the basis for these stereotypes? Do they apply to you?

EXPLORING STEREOTYPES

2D. STORY SHARING: HARD TIMES

Some people live daily confronted with stereotypes of the cultures they represent or the cultures that others assume they represent. Sometimes these assumptions or automatic associations have advantages, but very often they have disadvantages.

Sharing some of our stories of being stereotyped can help us understand better how people feel or what it might be like to live with the burden of cultural stereotypes constantly being applied to you. (This burden is sometimes referred to as "rep sweats," meaning the pressure or stress of being seen as a representative for an entire group.) Some people regularly experience microaggressions that result from typing and stereotyping.

> "For things to reveal themselves to us, we need to be ready to abandon our views about them."
> —Thich Nhat Hanh

Use the following story sharing prompts to open conversation and help each other understand different experiences of stereotyping and microaggressions.

- When have you been disadvantaged because of a stereotype that someone had of you, your family, your job, your looks, your age, your religion, your neighborhood, your weight, your health condition, your citizen status, your criminal record, your level of education, your accent, your [fill in the blank]?

- Have you experienced microaggressions?

- If you have a hard time coming up with an example of being stereotyped or being on the receiving end of microaggressions, what might that indicate?

- Which stereotypes of others seem hardest for you to get out of your head? Why do you think this is?

> "**Microaggressions** are the everyday verbal, nonverbal, and environmental slights, snubs, or insults, whether intentional or unintentional, which communicate hostile, derogatory, or negative messages to target persons based solely upon their marginalized group membership."
> —www.psychologytoday.com

2E. EXPLORING YOUR CULTURAL IDENTITY: AN ASSOCIOGRAM

A cultural associogram is a way to visualize how cultures are related or associated with one another in the life of a person. Describing or reflecting on an associogram for yourself can help you unpack a bit more who you are and why. This activity has three basic steps:

Step 1: Draw your associogram.

Step 2: Describe your different cultures and how they are related to one another.

Step 3: Reflect on how the cultures in your associogram influence you.

Consider the example below of Steps 1, 2, and 3, then sketch your own associogram and talk about it with someone else.

Example

Step 1: Draw your associogram. The visual below is a graphic showing how some of Penny's broad cultures, subcultures, and microcultures are related to one another.

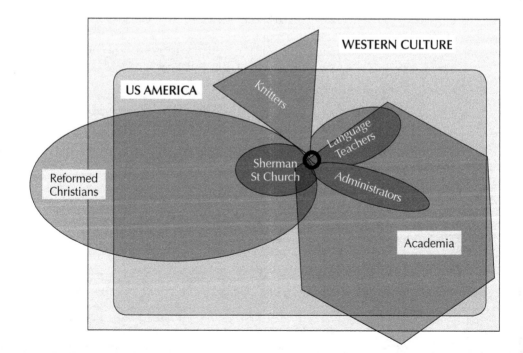

Step 2: Describe your different cultures and how they are related to one another.

- Western culture and US-American culture are my broad cultures. Almost everything I do is influenced by these two broad cultures.

- Academia and Reformed Christians represent subcultures that are key to who I am. For me, my academia subculture is mostly inside US-American and Western cultures. But I have spent some time as a professor in Germany, New Zealand, and Southeast Asia. I have had the opportunity to interact with Reformed Christians in Germany (outside US-American culture but still inside Western culture) as well as Reformed Christians in South Korea, Cambodia, and Thailand (outside US-American and Western cultures).

- I included four microcultures that are important to my identity: language teachers, administrators, Sherman St. Church, and knitters. Sherman St. Church is a microculture completely inside the Reformed Christians culture. Language teachers and administrators are for me microcultures inside academia. I would like to offer a class on knitting, but unfortunately, knitters is a microculture that I associate with neither academia nor Reformed Christians. I have connected with knitters in both Germany and New Zealand but not in Asia, so for me, this microculture extends outside US-American culture but not outside Western culture.

Even if another person chose the same cultures to visualize their cultural identity, they might place and overlap them differently.

Step 3: Reflect on how the cultures in your associogram influence you. Because I teach at a Reformed Christian university, the Reformed Christians culture overlaps with academia for me. I have many colleagues whose faith cultures and work cultures have very little overlap. In some ways, this overlap is a positive: I get to integrate faith very actively in much of my academic work.

I thought about my Asian roots and wondered if I should put myself on the border between two broad cultures: Eastern and Western. In the end, I decided that I am rooted very strongly in Western cultures and not so much in Eastern cultures and values. I guess this makes sense because I moved from Taiwan to the US when I was five years old. All my formal education has taken place in the US, where I have spent most of my life.

Knitters are a microculture. We have jargon such as entrelac, purling, and SSK; we use products such as double-pointeds and stitch holders; we practice things such as petting yarn and yarn bombing; and as a group, we value both creativity and following patterns. The process of producing a garment is as important as the final product. I suppose knitters have some of the same values and perspectives as other artisans or crafters: the time and attention put into an object makes it worth more, and one-of-a-kind pieces carry extra value.

Now it is your turn.

Step 1: Draw your associogram. Consider some of the broad cultures, subcultures, and microcultures that are important to your identity. Begin by identifying one to four cultures for each category below.

Broad Cultures	Subcultures	Microcultures

Next, sketch your associogram, overlapping and connecting cultures or keeping them separate as seems right to you.

Step 2: Describe your different cultures and how they are related to one another.

Step 3: Reflect on how the cultures in your associogram influence you. Talk about the three P's (products, practices, and perspectives) associated with the different cultures. Do the different cultures you belong to seem in tension or in harmony with one another? How much do your cultures overlap?

2F. ANALYZING LEVELS OF CULTURE: THE THREE P'S TOOL

PRODUCTS
PRACTICES
PERSPECTIVES

By looking more closely at the products, practices, and perspectives of a culture, and at how these different pieces fit together, you can deepen your understanding of the culture you are exploring. In fact, this type of exploration can help you discover important things about your own cultures and cultural identity.

Products
food,
festivals,
fairy tales

Practices
behaviors
etiquette

Perspectives
worldview
cultural values

For each item in the list below, decide if it is most helpful to think of the item as a product, a practice, or a perspective by putting a mark in the corresponding column.

	Product	Practice	Perspective
1. When possible, you should stay two feet or sixty centimeters away from another person.			
2. Working out (to be physically fit).			
3. Microwave pre-packaged frozen dinners.			
4. Being productive is important.			
5. Loyalty is a virtue.			

	Product	Practice	Perspective
6. The saying "Spare the rod, spoil the child."			
7. Breath mints.			
8. Going for the corner office. (Focusing on getting promoted or achieving a higher status in an organization or at work.)			
9. Nike.			
10. Different words for "friend," "close friend," and "very close friend."			
11. Eating lunch at your computer.			
12. Letting someone copy your homework.			
13. Time is measurable in units and talked about like a commodity.			
14. Watches.			
15. Individual strength and endurance are good things.			
16. The TV show *Sesame Street*.			
17. Executing a very long, detailed contract to conduct business.			
18. Skin-lightening products.			
19. Watching Fox News.			
20. Wearing a head-scarf/hijab.			

Connections or links among a product, a practice, and a perspective are not exclusive. Usually more than one product is linked to a practice. For example, many objects or products, not just one, are directly associated with Hanukah or with Easter. Likewise, several practices can reflect or be evidence for a key perspective in a particular culture. For example, going to the gym, choosing diet drinks and low-fat food options, and wearing Spanx might all be linked to the cultural value of health and fitness.

Questions to Consider

Can you describe a linked set of product, practice, and perspective from the list above or from cultures you have experiences with?

Can you describe the links between some of the elements at the surface (or at the top of the pyramid), just below the surface (in the middle), and at the deeper levels of a culture?

Optional challenge activity

Work with a partner to create a web of products, practices, and perspectives, starting with one practice (at the top of the page) or one perspective (at the bottom of the page) that seems relevant to your lives, the goals of your ICQ group, or the cultural mix in your communities.

2G. STORY SHARING: YOUR TRADITIONS

TRADITIONS AND CULTURAL IDENTITY

Family traditions are part of the cultures that shape us. Sharing some of our traditions helps us understand one another and our subcultures. Better still, if we add into our discussion a little dose of ICQ, we can gain new insights into our cultural identities. Break into small groups and use the following story sharing prompts to guide a discussion of family traditions.

- If you were asked to bring in an object that represented something important about yourself or your family, what would you choose? Tell a little about how this object relates to other objects, practices, or values in your life.

"Family traditions counter alienation and confusion. They help us define who we are; they provide something steady, reliable and safe in a confusing world."
—Susan Lieberman

- Think of a tradition in your family that is important or unusual. How does this practice link to other products, practices, or perspectives in your family?
- If you could suggest a tradition or a practice that would become part of the culture of the community you are building or working on, what would you choose and why? What might be some related objects or products that people would notice when they visited or observed your community? What would you hope were the underlying values or perspectives?

NEXT STEPS

Look back at your responses in activity 1F, "Story Sharing: Reflections on Community." How do these harmonize with the ideas that arose during the story sharing about traditions (activity 2G)? What could be some of the top common goals for the community you are hoping to improve or build?

"I CAN . . ." SELF-CHECK FOR CHAPTER 2

For each "I can" statement, indicate how much you agree with it by circling yes or no or by marking a spot along the yes–no line in the right column.

I can describe in a few sentences what is meant and not meant by "We are products of a culture."	Yes ---------------------- No
I can name a stereotype I have of others and that others might have of me or of one of the groups I belong to.	Yes ---------------------- No
I can explain briefly what the iceberg concept of culture is.	Yes ---------------------- No
I can give examples from my own life of a broad culture, a subculture, and a microculture.	Yes ---------------------- No
I can give an example of a product, a practice, and a perspective in my home culture.	Yes ---------------------- No
I can explain how products, practices, and perspectives can be linked.	Yes ---------------------- No

Notes

Quotations in Learning Kit 2 are taken from Thich Nhat Hanh, *Being Peace* (Berkeley, CA: Parallax Press, 1987), 42; and Susan Lieberman, *New Traditions. Redefining Celebrations for Today's Family* (London: Farrar, Straus and Giroux, 1991), 20.

Learning Kit 3
for Chapter 3

She, He, and They—
ICQ Interpretation

CHAPTER 3 SUMMARY

A useful way of thinking about cultural differences is to consider which elements are central or core to our identities, which are negotiable, and which are additional.

- **Core elements** are essential to who we are or want to be. They define us at a deep level.
- **Negotiable elements** are practices or perspectives that we prefer and may consider important, but we can do without them temporarily or perhaps even long term, if doing so is necessary for some good reason.
- **Additional elements** are parts of our habits of living that we can consider optional and less important to our identities.

Being aware of which practices and perspectives are core or negotiable for ourselves and others can help us better understand and interpret the differences. We can also reconsider our own flexibility: what is for us truly central and what can be negotiable or optional.

Cultural dimensions help us make sense of broad cultural differences. Although every culture has diversity within it, there are tendencies within a culture for expectations and values centered around cultural dimensions, such as the role of the individual or long-term versus short-term orientation. **Guiding orientations focus more on our personal subcultures and microcultures, the principles or orientations that guide us in our everyday lives.** Understanding more about both cultural dimensions and our own guiding orientations can help us explain and understand cultural differences and interpret better what people say and do and why.

RECALLING CHAPTER 3

1. Can you provide an example from your life or your family or your community in which something that was central to your identity shifted to be negotiable or something that was negotiable or additional became much more important or "core" to who you are?

2. How do your guiding orientations (for you and your family) harmonize with the mainstream or majority culture(s) around you?

3A. DETERMINING THE CORE OF YOUR IDENTITY

This exercise will help you think about the core, negotiable, and additional elements of who you are.

Step 1: Fill in the table below. You might write down a product (object), a practice (habit), or a perspective (belief or value). Some of the boxes might remain empty.

	Core	Negotiable	Additional
products (food, drink, clothing, or "things")			
practices (work, daily activities, or how you do things)			
perspectives (faith, spirituality, top priorities, or main goals in life)			

Step 2: Discuss with a partner how you filled in the table.

- How might the answers of your grandparents have been similar or different?
- Can you imagine any of the things you wrote down shifting to a different column in the future? Why or why not?
- If the members of your ICQ group are fairly similar to each other, which squares would likely have quite different answers if another group were to fill them in?
- If your ICQ group is quite diverse, how can knowing more about what others consider core and negotiable help you communicate, get along, and work better together to build community? How does the Three Circles of Cultural Identity Tool help you interpret or understand cultural differences in helpful ways?
- How can you sensitively find out more about what others consider part of their core? If your ICQ group has hopes or plans of engaging (reaching out to, hosting, interacting with) a specific other group, consider this question for your specific target group.

SHIFTS IN WHAT IS IMPORTANT

3B. STORY SHARING: CORE OR NEGOTIABLE

Here is the figure from chapter 3 that helps you consider what is central to who you are, what isn't, and how things can change categories over time.

Share a personal story of how something shifted from one category to another one (core, negotiable, or additional). This could be a family story about grandparents, parents, or yourself. Perhaps you have an example from a community you have been part of: a school board, a committee at work, a faith community, a sports team, etc. What prompted the shift? How did this change affect the culture of that group?

What shifts in how you categorize a practice or a perspective could help your community move forward, grow closer, or be more welcoming?

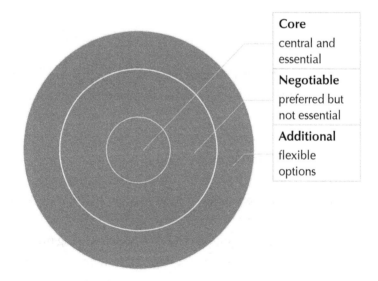

Core
central and essential

Negotiable
preferred but not essential

Additional
flexible options

3C. INTERPRETING DIFFERENCES: CASE STUDIES

Let's combine some of the tools to understand other people and other ideas better: in other words, to practice interpreting cultural differences. Work through the following exercises with one to three people.

Exercise 1

Name a product or a practice from your own life that you suspect plays a very different role for other people you know (the older/younger generation, your in-laws, or another subculture). Try to explain or interpret the cultural differences using the Three Circles of Cultural Identity Tool (pg. 45), the Cultural Dimensions Tool (pg. 50), and/or the My Guiding Orientations Tool (pg. 56).

Exercise 2

Below are cases of cultural differences. Choose one or two of the following and use the tools to interpret or explain the differences. If you feel you don't have enough knowledge to interpret well, how could you get more knowledge to help you interpret? Whom would you ask? Using the Hofstede cultural dimensions to compare Germany, France, and the US could be useful in your discussions.

> **Case A: Obeying crosswalk signs.** In German culture, pedestrians stand and wait for the pedestrian walk sign to turn green even if there is no car in sight. In downtown Boston, pedestrians rule the intersections and cross whenever they can and feel like it.

> **Case B: Not eating meat.** Karen is a vegetarian and a Seventh-Day Adventist versus Kyle, who is giving up meat for Lent and is a Baptist Christian.

> **Case C: Vacations and holidays.** Full-time employees in France are guaranteed five weeks of paid vacation in addition to the dozen public holidays and a maximum thirty-five-hour workweek. In the US, there is no mandatory guaranteed amount of paid vacation.

> **Case D: Public safety and lawsuits.** A person in the US wins a huge dollar settlement because Nutella chocolate hazelnut spread advertised itself

as part of a healthy breakfast. How would this play out in most of the rest of the world?

Case E: Recycling. Dividing household waste into different recycling, composting, and garbage containers is the law in Germany. Recycling is encouraged but not federal law in the US.

3D. INTERPRETING INTERCULTURAL SITUATIONS: EAST AND WEST

CULTURAL DIMENSIONS

Let's zoom in a little closer to examine how cultural dimensions and core values are linked to behaviors and expectations. We will build on the information about East and West in chapters 2 and 3. Take a look at the contrasting general descriptions of East versus West perspectives listed below, keeping in mind that these are generalizations and that within any culture there is diversity.

East Asians	Westerners
live in an interdependent world in which the self is part of a larger whole	live in a world in which the self is a unitary free agent
value success and achievement in good part because they reflect well on the groups they belong to	value success and achievement because they are badges of personal merit
value fitting in and engage in self-criticism to make sure they do fit in	value individuality and strive to make themselves look good
are highly attuned to the feelings of others and strive for interpersonal harmony as well as saving face in public	are more concerned with knowing themselves and are prepared to sacrifice harmony for fairness
are accepting of hierarchy and group control	are more likely to prefer equality and lots of latitude for personal action or decisions
avoid controversy and debate	have faith in the rhetoric of argumentation in arenas from law to politics to science

Richard Nisbett writes in *The Geography of Thought* that there are very dramatic social-psychological differences between East Asians as a group and people of European cultures as a group. Although the summaries of core values in chapter 3 and the differences in perspectives outlined in the table above are a simplified overview, how might you think differently about the following hypothetical situations with a little more ICQ? Let's assume there is a mix of East Asians and Westerners involved. **Choose at least one situation from each level below (personal, professional, and international) to discuss with a partner.**

In this discussion of possible cultural misunderstandings, we are trying to understand, from within its cultural context, something we notice as different. We are trying to explain, compare, and contrast our culture and the other culture in useful ways. We are practicing how to interpret this difference from within its cultural context and in a more informed way, aware of our own cultural perspectives. In other words, we are learning to shift from reacting to differences (cultural products, practices, and perspectives) from within one perspective (our own unanalyzed viewpoint) to using tools and knowledge about cultures and cultural identities to make useful comparisons and connections between cultures—i.e., to understand and interpret cultural differences better.

| Reacting without reflection or awareness of our own biases | Reacting from our perspective with some self-awareness | Interpreting by using skills and tools to compare differences |

For each of the situations below, try to describe the perspectives or motivations of each group (East Asians and Westerners). How might the different groups react, or why is there a potential for cultural misunderstandings?

Personal Level

- A mixed group of East Asians and Westerners goes to a restaurant. The oldest male orders for everyone without asking you what you want to eat.
- A parent mentions to a group of parents (mixed East Asian and Westerners) that her child did well at a school event.
- J. (with East Asian cultural ties) is invited to a party but never sends in his RSVP.
- X. (with East Asian cultural ties) serves a casserole and apologizes because it is probably not salty enough.

Professional Level

- The big contract in a multi-national company is given to the CEO's cousin.

- At a business meeting with a mix of East Asians and Western-ers, B. skips long introductions. After a quick welcome, he gets down to business by outlining the three big issues that need to be dealt with today.
- A company sends a new manager from the US to oversee a factory in China. He tries to make a good impression by being friendly with the workers on the floor and inviting the employees in his office out for drinks.

International Level

Based on this short introduction to East-West cultural dimensions, how might you look at the following international events or issues with new eyes? What might be the different perspectives you hadn't considered before? How might orientations or core values be playing out in the East-West discussions of these issues?

Sometimes good ICQ is demonstrated in being able to ask better questions. What pieces of cultural knowledge would you like to know?

- The EP3 spy plane incident in 2001. A US spy plane was forced by a Chinese piloted plane to make a crash landing in China. The US insisted that the Chinese pilot was at fault for forcing the US plane to crash. China demanded that the US admit it was spying (illegally) and apologize for the insult. Each country wanted the other to claim responsibility and apologize.
- Political protests in Hong Kong. In the "umbrella protest" in 2014, citizens protested proposed changes to the electoral system in Hong Kong, seen by some as interference by China's Communist Party in the leadership and elections in Hong Kong.
- The Chinese and US interpretations of human rights. Possible cases to discuss include China's ban on Facebook, the building of the Three Gorges Dam, the one-child policy, the arrest of artist Ai Weiwei, and the control of the media within China.

3E. STORY SHARING: YOUR COMFORT LEVEL

HOW DO YOU LIKE TO LEARN AND PROCESS?

How comfortable do you feel in this ICQ group? What would you like more of or less of in the ICQ group meetings?

Which statement (a, b, or c) in each group below is closest to how you feel related to some of the cultural orientations (from the short survey in chapter 3) or your personality tendencies (from activity 1B)?

Action: doing or being
- a. I like it best when we can come to a good conclusion together. I would like an action plan.
- b. I like the balance of personal learning at home, reflection, and discussion.
- c. I would like more time to get to know one another, go out for coffee, or watch films together.

Communication: instrumental or expressive
- a. I find the clear definitions and taking the surveys and applying a new idea to a concrete situation most helpful. I like analyzing the pros and cons.
- b. I like the at-home reading, learning about the big concepts, and also the learning and story times together as a group.
- c. I most like the stories and hearing about others' frustrations or experiences.

Fiery red, earthy green, cool blue, or sunshine yellow
- a. I like to process new ideas on my own or with just one other friend.
- b. I enjoy getting together with the ICQ group and discussing things altogether.
- c. During our ICQ group meetings, I like working with just a couple of other people to do a learning exercise or share our stories.

You can get a feel for the group results by a show of hands or "voting" with sticker dots on a large printout of the above statement options.

Is there strong consensus or diversity in the group results? What if any suggestions would you like to make for the remaining ICQ group meetings? If you did activity 1C, you might revisit your community ground rules. Are there any additions or edits you would like to make to those ground rules?

"If you feel comfortable 100% of the time, someone else is feeling uncomfortable 100% of the time."

—projected at the beginning of a worship service at Madison Square Church, Grand Rapids, Michigan

3F. LEARNING MORE ABOUT CULTURAL ORIENTATIONS

This survey is a slightly different and extended version of the one in chapter 3. How do individuals or even societies differ in terms of their overall orientation to the following eight themes?

* how we relate to the environment
* how we view our actions or activity
* our bias in how we reason
* our preference for communication styles
* the role of the individual in society
* the literal and figurative ideas of privacy
* our norms for operating in society (competition and cooperation)
* our tolerance for ambiguity or need for clarity and order

This survey can be used to consider how your guiding orientations are different from other people's or from the guiding orientations of the society or communities in which you live, work, worship, learn, etc.

The My Guiding Orientations Tool and the Cultural Dimensions Tool overlap in their themes. You can use the Cultural Dimensions Tool to focus on national or broad cultures. You can use the My Guiding Orientations Tool to focus on individuals, subcultures, and microcultures.

Idea 1: Complete the survey on your own. In which themes do you feel the most tension? In which orientations (environment, action, thinking, etc.) are you most different from others in your life or from your communities?

Idea 2: Work through the survey with a partner. Each person circles the number that corresponds to them personally. What do the similarities or differences in your answers mean for how you can best work together or with others?

Idea 3: If you like details and analyzing, work on aligning the themes from this guiding orientations survey with the six cultural dimensions.

For each spectrum described below, circle the number that matches where you would place yourself on that spectrum. Which phrase best describes your thinking or way of living? There are eight themes. Some themes have more than one question to help you try to figure out your orientation.

Environment: control, constraint, or harmony

Humans can control the environment; it can be changed to fit human needs.	Humans should live in harmony with the world around them.	Humans are constrained by the world around them. Fate, luck, and chance play a significant role.
7 6	5 (4) 3	2 1

Action A: doing or being

Accomplishing a goal or achieving a result is important. Productivity is highly valued.	7 6 (5) 4 3 2 1	The process and experience is more important than a specific accomplishment or product. Relationships are highly valued.

Action B: single-minded and down-to-business or multitasking and socially focused

I tend to concentrate on one task at a time. I generally live a very scheduled life and stick to my day planners.	7 6 (5) 4 3 2 1	I tend to concentrate on many tasks at once. I am more concerned about relationships than deadlines.

Thinking A: deductive or inductive

I value reasoning based on theory and logic.	7 6 5 (4) 3 2 1	I value reasoning based on experience and experimentation.

Thinking B: linear or systematic

I tend to think analytically and break problems into small components.	7 6 (5) 4 3 2 1	I tend to think holistically and focus on the big picture and the interrelationships among components.

Communication A: low context or high context

I believe people should be clear in exchanging facts and information.	(7) 6 5 4 3 2 1	I believe people shouldn't have to discuss everything explicitly. A lot of information is understood from the context.

Communication B: direct or indirect

I prefer explicit one- or two-way communication, including identification, diagnosis, and management of conflict.	7 (6) 5 4 3 2 1	I prefer implicit, intuitive communication and avoid conflict or direct confrontation.

Communication C: instrumental or expressive

I value unemotional, impersonal communication styles. Objectivity is good.	7 6 (5) 4 3 2 1	I value emotional, personal communication styles. Subjectivity makes the message real.

Communication D: informal or formal

One can easily dispense with ceremony and rigid protocol. A casual style seems personable.	7 (6) 5 4 3 2 1	It is important to follow protocol and social customs. Showing respect in how we speak is valued.

Individualism A: individualistic or collectivistic

The "I" predominates over the "we." I value independence.	7 6 5 4 (3) 2 1	Individual interests are subordinate to group interests. Identity is based on the social network, and loyalty is important.

Individualism B: particular or universal

It is important to consider changing circumstances and personal situations.	(7) 6 5 4 3 2 1	What is true, correct, and appropriate can be identified and applied to everyone. Societal obligations are important.

Space A: private or public		
I value personal space and prefer a bit of distance between myself and others.	7 6 (5) 4 3 2 1	I have less attachment to personal space and close proximity to others seems friendly and normal.

Space B: egalitarian or hierarchical		
I value minimizing differences in level or power or status. Dwelling on status is elitism.	7 6 5 (4) 3 2 1	I value the status differences between individuals or groups. Maintaining clear differences contributes to an orderly society.

Competitiveness: competitive or cooperative		
I value achievement, assertiveness, and material success.	7 6 5 4 3 (2) 1	I value quality of life, interdependence, and relationships.

Structure: order or flexibility		
I value predictability and rules.	7 6 5 (4) 3 2 1	I am tolerant of unpredictability and ambiguity.

The four spectrums related to communication (Communication A, B, C, and D) can be particularly useful as you start chapter 4, which focuses on interpersonal skills for interaction and dialogue.

3G. STORY SHARING: IMAGINING A NEW STORY

DEVELOPING A VISION

For this activity, you might focus first on this ICQ group and then on another target group or community you are interested in improving or building.

While we can understand in our heads that certain practices are negotiable pieces of our identities, we still like them because they make us feel comfortable. Unfortunately, in any diverse group (sometimes even in our own families), the same things do not make everyone feel comfortable.

- Which practices or products would make your target group feel comfortable, welcome, listened to, invited, and valuable (even if they might make you feel a little uncomfortable at the same time)?
- What needs to change in how you do things in order to foster or improve relationships in the community you are trying to build?

These conversation starters may help get the ball rolling.

- Perhaps we would feel more welcoming if . . .
- I might feel more at home if . . .
- I would like to learn more about . . .
- We could find out more by . . .
- It could be helpful to share . . .
- I wonder if things could really change by . . .
- What if we tried . . .

NEXT STEPS

Learning activity 1F, "Story Sharing: Reflections on Community" helped you dream about what your ideal communities might look like. What were the takeaways from those discussions?

Activities 3A, "Determining the Core of Your Identity," and 3B, "Story Sharing: Core or Negotiable," got you thinking about what you need to change or do to welcome others into relationships and community in culturally intelligent ways. What are the two or three things that are at the top of your to-do list?

Activity 3G, "Story Sharing: Imagining a New Story," will help you start planning. What concrete steps can you take toward becoming the community you dream of?

"I CAN . . ." SELF-CHECK FOR CHAPTER 3

For each "I can" statement, indicate how much you agree with it by circling yes or no or by marking a spot along the yes-no line in the right column.

I can explain what is meant by core, negotiable, and additional elements of a person's identity.	Yes --------------------- No
I can give an example of a core, negotiable, and additional element of my own identity.	Yes --------------------- No
I can describe briefly what some of the six cultural dimensions are and give an example of how cultures might be different regarding some of these dimensions.	Yes --------------------- No
I can describe how something that was core or negotiable in my cultures or personal life has shifted over time and is now in a different circle of cultural identity for me.	Yes --------------------- No
I can give an example of how differences in guiding orientations or core values might lead to a misunderstanding or an awkward situation.	Yes --------------------- No

Learning Kit 4
for Chapter 4

Me and You—
ICQ Interpersonal Skills

CHAPTER 4 SUMMARY

Interpersonal skills are a key component of intercultural skills. Although the details of how to navigate personal interactions may vary among cultures, ICQ interpersonal skills are learnable, awareness-building skills that can improve how we engage interpersonally across all kinds of lines of difference.

Four ICQ interpersonal skills are:
- openness
- observation
- flexibility
- empathy

These skills help us listen and read a situation, show respect and empathy appropriately, and interact and dialogue with others.

RECALLING CHAPTER 4

1. How can you show respect to people you engage with in your different communities or subcultures? What are some strategies for figuring out what behaviors, words, or even body language are respectful in other cultures?

2. What strategies can you use to be sure the amount of time you spend and your ways of listening and speaking are appropriate and well-balanced in your interactions with others?

4A. REVIEWING KEY IDEAS

Let's review the three ICQ skill areas and some of the key ideas thus far.

Warm-up

Which tools or big ideas of ICQ do each of these images represent?

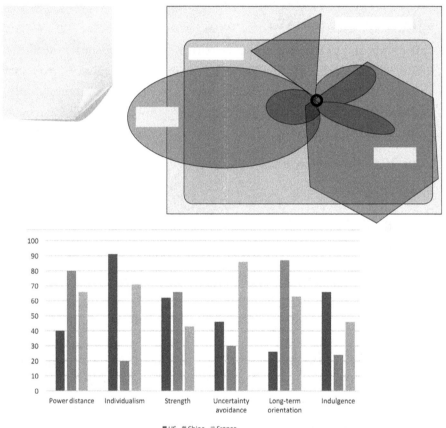

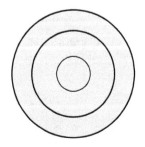

Exercise

Step 1: Divide into three small teams. Assign one column of terms and ideas in the table below to each team.

Chapter 2: ICQ Knowledge	Chapter 3: ICQ Interpretation	Chapter 4: ICQ Interpersonal Skills
• stereotypes • the Three P's Tool • broad cultures, subcultures, and microcultures	• Three Circles of Cultural Identity Tool • Six Cultural Dimensions Tool • My Guiding Orientations Tool	• openness • observation • flexibility • empathy

- Review together in your small team what you remember about the ideas or words in your column.
- Do you remember or have a concrete example or a story for one of the key ideas related to your column or chapter?

My small team focus is:

__ ICQ Knowledge   __ ICQ Interpretation   __ ICQ Interpersonal Skills

Key Ideas and Definitions	Concrete Example or Story That Illustrates a Key Idea

Step 2: Plan to share. Prepare a three- to five-minute review of the most important ideas from your assigned chapter to present to the entire ICQ group.

- What are the two or three most important ideas for everyone to remember?
- What concrete example could help people remember a key point or stay focused on the main ideas?

- Who will be the speaker for your group's shared review?

Step 3: Present the key ideas. Each small group has a few minutes to present the key ideas from their discussion. Focus on what is most important to remember about the topic or chapter you discussed.

4B. UNDERSTANDING YOUR INTERPERSONAL SKILLS

Take a few minutes to do the self-check below, which can help you think about your interpersonal skills. Of course, the following self-check will not measure you in any scientific way. But it will help you think about and discuss strengths, weaknesses, and where you are in your own development of ICQ interpersonal skills.

For each section, indicate how true the statements are for you most of the time. Don't overthink things. Just read each statement and circle a number along the scale from "very true" to "very untrue." This can be done altogether if one person reads each statement and pauses briefly for everyone to circle a number for that statement.

Openness	
I am curious. I love exploring. I always try new things. Taking risks is exciting.	very true < 5 4 3 2 1 > very untrue
I frequently invite people over to my home. I frequently have people (not family) stay overnight at my home.	very true < 5 4 3 2 1 > very untrue
I frequently watch foreign films, try new foods, and go to events to hear speakers or learn about topics I don't know much about.	very true < 5 4 3 2 1 > very untrue
Observation	
In an extended conversation with friends and family, I ask more questions than I answer from others.	very true < 5 4 3 2 1 > very untrue
I often read different blogs or listen to two or more different sources of news from diverse viewpoints.	very true < 5 4 3 2 1 > very untrue
I am keen to hear about and understand new ideas or opinions about international affairs or current events from a different religious perspective or from the perspective of other countries or cultures.	very true < 5 4 3 2 1 > very untrue

Flexibility	
I am willing to eat foods I hate in order to avoid making my host feel bad.	very true < 5 4 3 2 1 > very untrue
If I travel somewhere, I always check on the local expectations for clothing. I try to wear clothes appropriate for the local cultures (broad, sub-, micro-) even if they make me hot or uncomfortable.	very true < 5 4 3 2 1 > very untrue
I always ask about any food preferences when organizing food for a meeting or inviting people to eat with me at home or in restaurants.	very true < 5 4 3 2 1 > very untrue
Empathy	
I can understand how the actions of other countries can be logical within their set of cultural orientations or cultural values.	very true < 5 4 3 2 1 > very untrue
I have purposely tried to walk in the shoes or share the experiences of a person very different from me (in worship styles, religious practice, racial/ethnic background, citizen status, socioeconomic or educational background, etc.).	very true < 5 4 3 2 1 > very untrue
I can describe some of the key practices and perspectives of religious traditions different from my own. I can do this in a way that people from those other traditions would feel is fair. I have considered whether some of those other practices or perspectives might have benefits for me.	very true < 5 4 3 2 1 > very untrue

Now discuss the following questions with the group:

- Which interpersonal skills (openness, observation, flexibility, or empathy) seem to come naturally to you or are already something you are working hard at?
- Which interpersonal skill is perhaps most challenging for you or a skill area in which you have the greatest potential to grow?
- For the community that your group is focused on building or engaging with, which interpersonal skill seems to be a strength for your group and which is the area where growth is most needed?

4C. DIALOGUING ACROSS DIFFERENCES

ICQ interpersonal skills align with good dialogue goals. In fact, all the ICQ skills can help you in dialoging well with others. You can listen without judgment, listen to learn, share your stories, uncover more of your own identity and the identities of others, work to form community with the people involved, and challenge yourself and your preconceived notions of others. The table below aligns the ICQ interpersonal skills with the goals of good dialogue.

ICQ Interpersonal Skills	Good Dialogue Goals
Openness	Broadening your perspectives. Being open-minded to engage in dialogue. Being open to understanding other viewpoints.
Observation	Listening without judgment. Allowing for different opinions and experiences.
Flexibility	Enlarging and possibly changing or being flexible in how you see things. Expressing and exploring paradox and ambiguity.
Empathy	Finding common ground. Collaborating. Understanding.

Warm-up 1

Which interpersonal skill is needed most by each person in each situation below?

a. **Jordan** likes to wear muscle shirts, especially when it is hot outside. The family is leaving for the Fourth of July reunion picnic, and **his mother** asks him to put on nicer clothes. Jordan gets mad.

b. **Jamal** gets all his news from one source.

c. **Aminah** gets all her news from Facebook. She hates listening to **her uncle's** comments about politics because she and her uncle are on opposite sides of most issues.

d. **Kylie** is studying business at college. Her friend **Shawna** has a new baby. Kylie is going out with some friends for dinner. She knows Shawna would like to come too but isn't sure she wants to invite Shawna because all she wants to talk about is motherhood.

Warm-up 2

Using this rather superficial example, practice the four interpersonal skills. Joe and Lana are ordering takeout. Joe wants to order Chinese. Lana wants pizza. What kinds of questions, actions, or responses could each person have to show openness, observation, flexibility, or empathy?

Practicing ICQ Interpersonal Skills and Good Dialogue

Here are a few chances to practice good dialogue while using ICQ interpersonal skills. Choose one of the role-plays and act it out. After a couple of minutes, see if you can analyze what went well and what could have gone better with a different approach, a different response, or use of one of the interpersonal skills.

> **Role-Play A: hunting.** Eric loves hunting. He wants to take his fifteen-year-old nephew, Javon, along so they can spend time together doing something he loves. Javon's parents aren't sure about introducing Javon to hunting. Play these roles: the uncle Eric and one of the parents.
>
> **Role-Play B: the New Year's Eve party.** The Joneses always have a party for the neighborhood on New Year's Eve at which they serve alcohol. The Azari family moves into the neighborhood. They are Muslim. Play these roles: an adult member of the Jones family and of the Azari family talking about the upcoming neighborhood New Year's Eve party.
>
> **Role-Play C: changing the time of the worship service.** In a worshiping community, the younger families and people want to move the start time later. The older families and people want to keep the start time earlier. Play these roles: a representative from each side talking about the best action for the situation.

4D. ANALYZING A MIXED CULTURE SITUATION

Here is where the rubber meets the road, as they say. Your facilitator will organize the ICQ group into small teams and will choose a situation for you to analyze in those small teams. Each team receives one commercial or story to analyze. They can be found at the end of this activity.

Step 1: Analyze the situation. View or read together your assigned commercial or story. Here is what you are looking for: What parts of ICQ are being done (well) or are missing? Different persons or players in the situation might be demonstrating (or not) different parts of ICQ. Discuss together what you see and your evidence for your conclusions. Here are some reminders to focus your analysis.

ICQ Knowledge	ICQ Interpretation	ICQ Interpersonal Skills
• Recognizing stereotypes • Understanding that we are products of our cultures • Knowing about the products, practices, and perspectives of a culture	• Considering the core, negotiable, and additional parts of our cultural identities • Understanding how cultures, especially broad cultures, differ in cultural dimensions • Considering how individuals differ in guiding orientations	• Being open to learning from others, tuning in to situations, being aware of the need for ICQ • Observing actively and asking questions • Trying to be flexible • Seeking to understand others, their perspectives, and their motivations

Step 2: Prepare an ICQ-building analysis. Work with your small team to prepare your insights related to your assigned situation. Assign one person to present your answers to these questions.

- What was done well in the situation?
- Who showed or missed the opportunity to show ICQ?
- What could have been done better with some ICQ (knowledge, interpretation, and/or interpersonal skills)?
- How would your team advise someone in a similar situation? Or what can we learn from this situation?

Step 3: Present the analysis. Each small team first plays or describes the video or reads aloud the story for everyone. Then the small team member presents the team's analysis using the questions in step 2.

Step 4: Debrief with the entire group. What insights or strategies for intercultural interactions did you learn from each of the small teams and their situation analysis?

Sample Situations

There are two sets of situations: set 1 contains three TV ads for the HSBC bank; set 2 contains first-person stories. The facilitator should assign one commercial or story to each small team. The number of situations used will depend on the size of the entire ICQ group, the desired size of the small teams, and the amount of time you wish to devote to this activity.

Set 1: HSBC Intercultural Commercials

Google these HSBC ads or find them at https://www.youtube.com/watch?v=GOHvMz7dl2A. The commercials can be streamed during the ICQ team meetings if internet or data streaming is available, or they can be secured in advance.

- HSBC Culture Ad Subway
- HSBC Culture Ad Soup
- HSBC Culture Ad Golf

Set 2: Intercultural Stories

Each of these stories is told in the first person and is an experience of a real person.

A. Dressed Down

I was super excited to go to Cambodia on a month-long study trip with my college. We were warned that although January is winter in Cambodia, the temperatures would be in the 80s or 90s, hot and humid. So glad I wasn't there in the "hot" season. When we visited a nongovernmental organization (NGO) working on clean water issues, we learned a great deal about the role of education, local leadership, and sustainable development. But what I will never forget is how the NGO director yelled at us for how we were dressed. It was so hot. We were a bunch of college students, so we were wearing shorts, tank tops, and some spaghetti straps. He said we didn't look at all like nice young Christians, rather the opposite. It wasn't like we were all going to go buy a new wardrobe halfway through the month.

B. "Have Some Coffee"

I do not care for coffee; however, if pressured, I will drink it. Being a missionary in Costa Rica, where coffee is king, often put me in an awkward position. When I was offered a cup of coffee, I declined. But since the working assumption is that everyone always wants coffee, polite hosts frequently poured a cup and handed it to me, and I drank it.

> *"Greetings! I am pleased to see that we are different. May we together become greater than the sum of both of us."*
>
> —Surak in the *Star Trek* episode "Savage Curtain"

I was often in the home of Juan Carlos and Gloria, a pastor and his wife. On these visits, Gloria always asked if I cared for a cup of coffee, and I invariably asked instead for water or some other cold drink. Finally, Gloria confronted me. Her friend Margarita had told her that I always drank coffee at her (Margarita's) house. Gloria wanted to know why I never drank her own coffee. I explained that when I am asked, I always refuse, but Margarita never asks. She just pours the coffee and hands it to me.

Gloria was very pleased to hear that explanation. She had worried that Margarita's coffee was better. Now that she knew the real reason, she was more than content. From that day on, every time I visited Gloria's house, she prepared a cup of coffee and handed it to me without asking. I always drank it.

C. Cultural Bias in Textbooks

When you start learning a foreign language, you often talk about traveling and vacations. "Describe a memorable family vacation or trip" is a common assignment at some point in Spanish or French or German 101. I assigned this topic almost every year until Jamal. "Professor," he confided, "my family never went on vacations."

"Any interesting trips?" I asked. "Visiting family or friends?"

Jamal shook his head. "We pretty much just stayed in town."

I realized the bias built into my curriculum and the topics handled in many of the language textbooks. They assumed most people had majority culture, middle- or upper-middle-class childhood experiences: What do your parents do for a living? Describe your family's house. Tell about a memorable family vacation. The textbooks provided speaking and writing assignments and lovely vocabulary lists to allow learners to talk about those things. But Jamal did not have many of those memories to talk or write about. His experiences were equally interesting but just not covered by the curriculum.

D. You or You?

Like several memorable older German women I have known, Frau Strube had opinions, was direct, and loved her flowers. Her stories of life in former East Germany and her losses before and after German reunification underscored her resilience. When I stayed with her while doing a teacher training seminar in Leipzig, I cooked several dinners for her and she served up some fine European breakfasts.

A couple times I slipped up and used "du" with her. What is that? In German, as in many languages, there are different words for "you," depending on who it is. In general, "du" is for a person you know well, such as close friends, children, family, pets, and God. In contrast, "Sie" is for persons not inside your friend or family group, for more formal relationships or situations in which maintaining personal distance is deemed important. After Frau Strube shared with me about losing her husband and invited me around 11 p.m. onto her balcony to see a flower that blooms only one night each year, I very much wished to use "du" with her. She had changed from the woman I boarded with into someone I was quite fond of. What stopped me? She was much older than I was, and I figured she was the one who really had to initiate a conversation about switching from Sie (formal) to du (familiar).

When I left, we hugged, and I'm pretty sure I saw tears in her eyes. She pointed a finger at me a little accusingly. "I'm going to miss you." The German friends who picked me up noticed and thought the obvious bond was quite unusual. "Yes," I agreed. "But I'm sort of sad she never said that we could use "du" with each other."

"Oh no," my friend countered. "*You* are the one who has to initiate that switch." This did not make sense to me, because I was so much younger than Frau Strube. "You're the professor with the PhD and the paying boarder. Status trumps age." In case this isn't clear, in Germany, being a professor is very high on the social status scale—very different from in the US, in my experience. Funny how I actually have to remember and get used to that.

E. "Hay campo!" ("There's room!")

Our local church in Los Guido, Costa Rica, planned a river baptism and picnic. Very few members owned vehicles, so those of us who did have vehicles agreed to drive as many people as we could.

When the congregation gathered around the cars, it was immediately clear that one or two of the vehicles would have to make two trips in order to transport all the people. We decided to take as many people as possible on the first trip so that as few people as possible would miss out on the beginning of the festivities.

My wife and I drove a Nissan Vanette (a light version of a van), with seating for a driver and eight passengers. Given that space, nine adults got in. They then called to those remaining outside, "Hay campo!" ("There's room!") Eight children got in to sit on the laps of the adults. They then called to those remaining outside, "Hay campo!" ("There's room!") Each time they called out, more children climbed in, including a group of youths who stood in the luggage slot right behind the last row of seating.

My wife was nervous. No seatbelts—well, at least not twenty-two of them. Dirt roads full of potholes. What if the van's suspension gave out?

Meanwhile, the same process was going on in the other vehicles. With twenty-one passengers in our eight-passenger van, plus the driver, and similar overloads in the other vehicles, the entire congregation traveled to the river with none left behind waiting for a driver to return for a second trip.

4E. APPLYING ICQ SKILLS

This is a chance to imagine what it could look like to navigate in an ideal way a situation in which cultures are coming into contact. Sometimes figuring out a way forward is harder than analyzing what other people are doing right or wrong (which is what you did in 4D).

Choose a situation from the list below or come up with your own—something relevant to your contexts. Then build a small group with others interested in the same or a similar topic. For each row in the case study guide below, consider together good questions to ask, helpful ways to think about the situation, or useful next steps. In each situation, your goal is to end up in a better place or space, in other words, to build or improve the relationships in the situation, so that you can move forward in your journey together.

1. Your sister (or sister-in-law, friend, coworker) is really getting into yoga, meditation, and exploring Eastern religions and philosophies. You want to understand her new passion (and person) better.

2. Your son (or daughter, niece, nephew, grandchild, young person you care for) is hanging out more and more with some people you do not know, and you are a little worried.

3. Your parents (or grandparents, adults you live with) do not approve of or appreciate your friends, your way of dressing, or your music (or all of the above).

4. The new significant other in your extended family is from a different faith tradition than most or all of the rest of your family.

5. At your work (or moms/parents group, worshiping community, school, club), there are many people from one socioeconomic and/or religious and/or racial-ethnic background and only a few from a different one. Since you recently completed this ICQ book group, you have been tapped as a diversity and inclusion ambassador.

Case Study Guide

ICQ Skill area	Questions to ask, helpful ways to think about the situation, or useful next steps
ICQ Knowledge	
ICQ Interpretation	
ICQ Interpersonal Skills	
Your strategies, next steps, ways forward, approaches, questions, possible actions	

4F. STORY SHARING: UNDERSTANDING AND APPRECIATING DIFFERENCES

Quick Opinion Questions

- What makes a person difficult to like?
- What makes someone hard to get along with?

Partner Discussion

1. Share your answers to the above questions.

2. Analyze your responses together using ICQ interpersonal skills (openness, observation, flexibility, empathy) or using the My Guiding Orientations Tool, focusing especially on the following themes:
   - doing < > being
   - linear < > systematic
   - instrumental < > expressive
   - competitive < > cooperative

3. Although you listed things that drive you crazy about some people, what could be the upside or benefits of the way those other people go about doing things?

4. Consider the following questions:
   - What is one of the difficult differences between you and someone else in your life (a child, a parent, a sibling, a friend, a coworker, a teammate, etc.)?
   - How might you work to understand the difference(s) in helpful ways?
   - What could be one potentially positive next step to take to improve this connection, the situation, or your own understanding and strategies for interacting with this person?

(DIS)COMFORT IN INTER-PERSONAL SITUATIONS

4G. STORY SHARING: LEARNING TOGETHER FROM OUR EXPERIENCES.

In groups of three to five people, use some of the story sharing prompts below to encourage sharing from your experiences. Not everyone has to share a story, but everyone should speak either in sharing or in encouraging others by responding or asking a follow-up question to someone's story.

- Tell about a time when you were in a mixed culture/subculture or new situation and felt uncomfortable.
- Recount an experience in which you or someone else seemed to be particularly weak in interpersonal skills or in which someone demonstrated particularly strong interpersonal skills.
- Recall an awkward conversation at work or school or in your everyday life when you were at a loss for words or you said or did something you wish you could take back or when someone else said something you felt was inappropriate.
- Describe an intergenerational issue or tension (possibly in your family) that you suspect or think is related to the different subcultures (orientations and core values) of each generation.

Sample Encouraging Responses
- Your story helps me understand ___ a little bit better.
- I appreciate hearing about . . .
- I'm sorry that happened to you.
- I hope I would act/react in a good way in that situation.
- It would be interesting to know more about . . .
                              how you felt.
                              what happened next.
                              what you wish had been said.

> Share a story. Change the world—
> one listener at a time.
> - family saying

Sample Follow-up Questions

- How would you do things differently now (with more ICQ)?
- What question would you like to ask . . .

  that person?
  an insider to that other group?
  an intercultural expert?

- Has anyone else had a similar experience?

NEXT STEPS

Below is a short list of possible next steps for ICQ building and, in particular, practicing ICQ interpersonal skills.

Form small groups. Each group chooses one concrete idea to brainstorm about, perhaps sparked by the suggestions 1 and 2 below.

Suggestion 1. Organize a panel discussion or a lecture/presentation and invite people to share their experiences, perspectives, and stories. These people could be:

- recent immigrants or refugees
- #blacklivesmatter organizers
- people from cultural centers in your community (Islamic, Jewish, Turkish, Hispanic, etc.)
- local religious leaders
- local or regional experts on intercultural training or on specific cultures

Tip: Focus first on openness and observation, in other words, listening and learning. An invitation to learn from another person should not have the hidden agenda of telling them what you think, or converting them, or pointing out how they are wrong and you are right.

Tip: Consider good ground rules for the audience so that the speaker feels welcome and respected. Consider how you can grow in flexibility and empathy.

Suggestion 2. Explore options for being a guest in other spaces and places.

- Request a tour and introduction to another religion and house of worship.
- Organize a field trip to a museum, installation, exhibit, or cultural celebration that can help you learn about and understand another people group better.

Tip: Ask an insider in advance for advice on how to show respect. Remember, you are not engaging in their space in order to understand how right your ideas are in comparison. Rather, you are there to learn from them about their products, practices, and perspectives—to understand what is important to them in their cultural context and why.

Tip: Develop a helpful guide for your team to promote good observation, conscious flexibility, and empathy during the event.

Use this table to guide your brainstorming and capture your insights.

Facts to Be Gathered	Questions to Ask or Issues to Be Aware Of	Strategies for Using Good Interpersonal Skills

Tip: Make a concrete list: What would you need to do to make these ideas happen?

If your ICQ group organizes a learning event like those suggested above, consider creating a time to debrief your learning opportunity as an ICQ team.

- What did you learn? What did you enjoy? What made you feel uncomfortable?
- What did you feel or think, wonder about, or question as you were learning?

- What would you like to know more about (but perhaps you weren't sure it was appropriate to ask)?
- Do you feel that the team or you personally listened well, showing respect and interest in appropriate ways?
- If you hosted guests, how did you make them feel welcome and respected? How did you or could you express or extend appreciation to them?
- If you were guests somewhere, did you feel the hosts were hospitable? How did you or could you express or extend appreciation to them?

"I CAN . . ." SELF-CHECK FOR CHAPTER 4

For each "I can" statement, indicate how much you agree with it by circling yes or no or by marking a spot along the yes-no line in the right column.

I can list and briefly describe the four ICQ interpersonal skills.	Yes ---------------------- No
I can explain why interpersonal skills are important for relationship building.	Yes ---------------------- No
I can give some examples of how a lack of interpersonal skills can make relationships difficult to nurture or maintain.	Yes ---------------------- No
I can talk about which interpersonal skills are easier for me and which skill areas I can grow or improve most in.	Yes ---------------------- No
I can identify an example of how I might be flexible in an intercultural situation.	Yes ---------------------- No

Notes

The quotation in Learning Kit 4 is taken from *Star Trek,* season 3, episode 22, "Savage Curtain," directed by Herschel Daugherty, written by Gene Roddenberry, aired March 7, 1969, on NBC.

Learning kit 4D: The Intercultural Story A is based on the experiences of a student group led by David Dornbos and Leonard De Rooy. Stories B and E were written by Robert Rienstra. C and D were written by Pennylyn Dykstra-Pruim. Used with permission.

Learning Kit 5
for Chapter 5

Working on Us—Acting, Reacting, and Our Overall Approach

CHAPTER 5 SUMMARY

Improving how we act and react in intercultural situations involves knowing how expectations or rules of behavior differ across cultures. For example, how to be polite or what being on time means is not the same in every culture. **We can navigate cultural differences by asking insiders, reflecting on what others are doing, and adapting our behaviors as appropriate or needed**.

We can think about our strategy for or approach to engaging with people different from us in two ways: as a tourist and as a sojourner.

- We can do things that bring us into contact with others but mostly for self-focused reasons and at a superficial level, a bit as a tourist might. Or we can engage more deeply with an interest in relationships and understanding, more as a sojourner or someone looking to really get a feel for or understand a different place or culture might.
- An important part of a sojourner experience is engaging with ICQ so that we can ask good questions, be good guests and hosts, and create for ourselves and others a sense of belonging.

Hospitality and belonging are central to community building.

- Being welcoming involves making others feel that they have a voice and a contribution to make to the community.
- When we open our hearts to make space for others and their stories, we participate in a metaphorical embrace that can change us.

ICQ helps us build relationships across cultural lines. This work is not easy, but we need to commit to it in order to reap the benefits: the ability to better understand ourselves and the world in which we live, to improve how we navigate our differences, and to create more welcoming communities that benefit from the strong relationships that connect the different groups.

RECALLING CHAPTER 5

1. Which products or practices make you feel comfortable when you are invited into a new situation?

2. What do you think are the biggest roadblocks that might prevent you from building relationships across cultural lines?

5A. UNDERSTANDING DIFFERENT WAYS OF BEHAVING

RULES AND EXPECTATIONS

Different cultures do things differently. Yet all cultures have ways of showing respect, exchanging information, affirming relationships, expressing appreciation or gratitude, and negotiating meaning. The following lighthearted exercise highlights different ways of behaving and also our underlying preferences for having things our way.

With a small group of partners, complete each statement or answer the question, coming up with at least two options or responses for each.

1. A proper meal begins with ____ and ends with ____.

2. A comfortable distance for the space between my nose and the nose of the person I am speaking with is _____.

Try this out with each other if you are not sure what your preferences are. Actually using a tape measure to figure out the distances at which you feel comfortable, somewhat uncomfortable, and very uncomfortable can be fun, funny, and informative.

3. If I am invited to someone's home for dinner (not a best friend but someone I am just getting to know), should I bring anything? If I should, what is appropriate and what is not?

4. An effective presentation includes the following:
   a. Don't begin with the main point. Talk around the main point in several ways so that when you state the main point at the end, it seems inevitable.

> *"I want you to know that a third of the people on this planet eat with their spoons and forks like you, a third of the people eat with chopsticks, and a third of the people eat with fingers like me. And we're all just as civilized."*
>
> —a stranger in Afghanistan talking to Rick Steves

    b. Begin with the main point and an outline of what you're going to say. Then fill in the outline.

    c. Begin with a story that grabs attention. End by returning to the story you began with.

    d. ...?

5. If you were told that you were going to meet and have dinner with the king or queen of England, how would you prepare? Could any similar strategies be useful as you prepare to meet, engage with, or work with people from another culture or community?

Now answer these questions:

- Do you agree on the best answers?
- Are you familiar with other cultures or subcultures in which the answers would be different?

5B. STORY SHARING: FIGURING OUT THE RULES

LEARNING FROM MISTAKES

Sometimes differences in expectations are highlighted when different cultures or sub-cultures or even families try to do something together. Occasions when you need to navigate different cultural expectations can include weddings, birthday parties, holiday gatherings, gift giving occasions, and attending a worship service or other faith-related events. Changing jobs or schools, joining a new club or team can also mean learning how to be a good employee, co-worker, or member in your new context.

Do you have an interesting experience or insight related to figuring out or misunderstanding social rules?

- Oops! When did you do the wrong thing? What did you learn from that experience?
- Ah! Do you have a success story of a time when you were not sure what the social rules were and you managed to navigate the situation well?

If you have a story that might help the group laugh together or cry together, or might just serve as an example of the honest struggle of engaging across lines of difference, consider sharing it.

What can we learn by sharing our stories of successes and failures when engaging across cultural lines?

> *"Knowledge rests not upon truth alone,*
> *but upon error also."*
> —Carl Jung

5C. ASKING GOOD QUESTIONS: SOJOURNER VS. TOURIST

Making a distinction between being a tourist and being a sojourner does not mean that all the tourist things are wrong. The tourist is focused on the adventure or relaxation, entertainment, souvenirs, selfies, and fun. The sojourner is looking to learn about and understand people who are different from them and perspectives different from their own, to grow their understanding of how life is lived in this world. It is helpful to be aware of when we are in tourist mode and when we are in sojourner mode. In any case, we should consider our own motivations for engaging in or with other cultures.

This exercise tunes your mind and heart to look and listen more like a sojourner. The list below includes brief descriptions of postcards or photographs. (The descriptions are not objective. Can you pick out words or phrases that could indicate a bias?) For each item, discuss together in small groups how you might use the described image as a springboard for more learning, for building your ICQ with a more sojourner approach. The list starts out light and moves toward more challenging issues. Use these questions to guide your discussion.

- What questions should you be asking?
- Which tools might help you analyze and understand the situation?
- Where might you go for stories and perspectives to help you understand more?

Image 1 (from Facebook): A crowd of young people is moving around chaotically. They seem lost. They are wearing long robes. Some are happy. Some are sad.

Image 2 (from Snapchat): A large bowl of slimy-looking goo is surrounded by plates loaded with something that looks like white cubes with black polka-dots and with things that look like yard grubs.

Image 3 (Cambodia): A happy Buddha statue is sitting next to a hotel reception desk. In front of the statue are a cup of coffee, a bowl of rice, and a plate of fruit.

Image 4 (Germany): A line of brightly costumed people wearing rather scary face masks are parading down a street. In the foreground, a man in a jester hat is blowing confetti into the face of a person in the crowd.

Image 5 (Thailand): Men with shaved heads wearing bright orange robes are accepting coins from locals, but the men in robes look well off and the locals look poor.

Image 6 (New Zealand): A banner that is eight feet wide and two stories tall is hanging on the wall of a building. It is covered completely with red flowers made of yarn, felt, and fabric. A person standing in front of the banner looks upset or sad.

Image 7 (from Al Jazeera): A man with a black scarf wrapped around his head is holding a gun in the air. The ruins of a town dominate the background. There is a dead body in the foreground.

Image 8 (from NPR): A helicopter is hovering over a boat in the water. Hundreds of people are crowded on the boat. They look poor and sick.

Image 9 (from CNN): A crowd of people is moving down a street. They are shouting. Along one side stands a row of police officers. In the background, flames are coming out of a building.

5D. PUTTING ICQ INTO ACTION

Work with a partner to apply your ICQ to some of the following situations. Each set of partners can be assigned two or more of the situations. Consider which situation seems most challenging for you and why. For each situation, answer these questions:

- What is your first reaction?
- What is your second reaction: what would you say or do?
- What knowledge or facts would you like to know?
- What would you try to observe or reflect on?
- What question would you ask and whom would you ask to help you interpret or negotiate the situation in the best possible way?

1. Your ten-year-old nephew asks if your Vietnamese neighbors speak Chinese.

2. You want to learn how to make authentic tamales. You would like to ask Viviana Gomez, who works in the office down the hall, but you are not sure if that is weird or making assumptions.

3. You just signed up to spend a week volunteering in a disaster relief area in a region far away from your home turf.

4. In a town-hall meeting in one of the communities you are connected to, you notice that one viewpoint is definitely louder and getting more airtime.

5. Your worshiping community would like to reach out to a neighborhood public school.

6. Your ICQ group (or another group you are in) is considering a "Service Saturday" to do good for a neighborhood, organization, or group of persons.

7. Your son/daughter has an open house or party to mark an important occasion (bar mitzvah, high school graduation, confirmation, etc.). You know that some of his/her friends who will attend are from a different cultural/ethnic or religious background.

8. At a family reunion, Uncle Martin tells a joke that plays off current race issues in the US or that makes a specific ethnic group the butt of the joke.

9. Your son/daughter/niece/nephew appears for departure to some event dressed in a way you feel is completely inappropriate.

10. At a family reunion or office party, someone brings a new significant other who appears to be from a different racial/ethnic background from everyone else.

Share insights or remaining questions you have with the entire group.

> *"Our world is changing rapidly, calling for new skills and knowledge in order for us to survive and prosper. Because of the interactions between nations and ethnic groups, our skills in forming and maintaining relationships with those who are culturally different from us will be critical for our success in the new millennium."*
> —Patty Lane

HOSPITALITY

5E. SHARING STORIES, DREAMS, AND BIG IDEAS

In English we have the Greek word *xenophobia*—the fear of strangers. In the Christian Bible there is a partner word: *philoxenia*—the love of strangers. You might recognize pieces of this Greek word in "**Phil**adelphia," the city of brotherly love, and "**xeno**phobia," the fear of strangers. *Philoxenia* is often translated by the word "hospitality."

In this activity, you are looking at how to be more welcoming. Start with story sharing and then move to a group exercise.

Story Sharing: Belonging or Not

Think back to a time where you felt welcomed, perhaps into a new class or club, a family, a job, a town. What concrete things made you feel welcome? In that new context, did you right away or at some point finally feel that you belonged? If yes, what contributed to that feeling of belonging? If no, what would have helped you feel like you did belong?

The Dream

Focus either on this ICQ group or on the communities or cultures that you are looking to engage with. Imagine the future and you are celebrating a wildly successful three-year journey building ICQ and community (or whatever length of time seems best). What does this community look like? What are the products, practices, and perspectives that characterize this dream space and place? Have each person say one statement that describes the dream. An individual may say "pass" if he or she wishes.

> Curiously in English we still have the word for fearing strangers but have lost the word for loving them.
> —Christians and Cultural Difference

If your team did activity 1G, how do your dreams now compare to the mission or vision statements you drafted earlier?

What If . . .?

How can you work toward realizing at least parts of your dream for a stronger, culturally intelligent community in which relationships across lines of difference are many and vibrant? Start a list of ideas on how to get to this point.

Encourage each person to complete one of these statements:

- What if . . . ?

- How about . . . ?

- Yes, and . . .

5F. CREATING PATHS THROUGH STORY

SHARING YOURSELF THROUGH STORIES

In this ICQ for community building project, you have acquired tools and a vocabulary to help you work better with others on cross-cultural understanding and relationship building. Here are a set of starter questions to open up good conversations for understanding people different from you; these create opportunities to hear one another's stories. You might use these questions to further explore the different cultures represented in your ICQ book group or you can take these questions with you as you reach out to or engage with other cultures in your community.

1. Who are the heroes of your community or culture or of you personally? Tell some of their stories. What core values are embodied in these heroes and stories?

2. What traditions does this community or culture really value? Describe some of the related practices and their importance, in other words, the perspectives or values they point to.

3. How does this community or culture love to have fun or be entertained? What products and practices are part of these times?

4. If you had to describe three perspectives that are central or core to the identity of this community, culture, or most of the people in it, what would they be? Are there some characteristics, perspectives, or practices that are in flux—that are in transition somewhere between core and negotiable within the identity of the community or culture?

5. What was a wonderful event or great success that this community or culture experienced recently? What made it wonderful, great, or successful? Which products, practices, and perspectives were showcased in the event?

Which of these five suggestions for inviting stories do you like best? Can you think of another focus or theme that could be a good way to create an opportunity to build relationships by sharing stories?

You might use these questions with mixed culture groups that you are trying to bring together. What type of event could work well for your situation?

- a panel discussion event
- a video interview series
- a cake-and-conversation event at which different persons from different cultures share pieces of their stories
- other?

Always remember that the stories or perspectives of any one person from a group is one piece of the rich mosaic of that culture or community.

5G. DOING AND BEING TOGETHER: IDEAS FOR A NEXT EVENT

As you conclude this ICQ for community building learning experience, it is time to look ahead. What can you do to use the tools you have been learning about and to keep the momentum going? The activities that student or youth groups often turn to in order to bring people together are still great ideas: faith-centered activities, celebrations, common causes (political, civic, educational, community improvements), service or volunteer opportunities. The difference now is that you are a little better equipped to build relationships with people who aren't already long-standing friends, to reach outside the group of people similar to you, and to grow.

Here are a few types of events or adventures that can become occasions for people from different cultures or communities to practice being together. These examples offer a fairly unthreatening environment combined with an opportunity for everyone to learn something new. Also, these suggestions allow you to continue building your ICQ about other cultures and communities as you work on your skills for engaging personally with them.

Have each small team choose one of the options below and brainstorm questions, ideas, and key insights. One way to brainstorm is for each team to produce a word cloud by putting the big idea in the middle of a large piece of paper and then adding helpful words, questions, or ideas around it.

Idea 1: The Global Kitchen Club

Eating together in restaurants or having a menu catered is a great way to bring people together. This can be a tourist experience, or you can turn it into an ICQ community building event by inviting the owner or the chef to tell their stories related to the food and to describe the traditions and cultures, the histories and perspectives surrounding the dishes you are eating. (The Global Kitchen Club is a social enterprise founded by Leah Selim that promotes cross-cultural understanding through kitchen diplomacy. They organize and host immigrant-led cooking classes and festive cross-cultural meals in New York City. For those interested in more information, her work is accessible on the internet through a TED Talk, articles, presentations, and various forms of social media.)

Idea 2: A Cook-in

Organize a cook-in with a mixed group of people. Invite someone from another culture or subculture to teach the group how to prepare traditional dishes from their home culture or tradition. Encourage story sharing around the holidays or traditions connected to the foods.

Idea 3: "Movies, Meanings, and More" or "Popcorn with a Purpose"

Films offer us glimpses into other parts of the world, our societies, and the human experience. Hosting film nights can also bring strangers together for fun and popcorn. Such an event can become a culture learning event if you carefully select films that highlight new or different perspectives or that inform you about other people's cultures and lives. Inviting insiders to facilitate a conversation about the film can help further the ICQ learning for everyone. Choose your films carefully. Consider some of the films listed in the notes and resources at the end of each chapter. In any case, consult with cultural insiders from the cultures represented or referenced in the film for input on the value of the film and how to process the film's messages appropriately.

Idea 4: Culture Explorations

You can learn more about other peoples and cultures in your communities by exploring together.

- Attend or participate in a cultural event different from the ones you usually attend. Have an insider provide an introduction, and then develop a helpful guide for your team to promote good observation and empathy during the event.
- Partner with a different group by setting up pen pals. Begin with an exchange of emails or letters. Encourage each pair to meet once in a neutral space for coffee, tea, or another drink. Then promote an event that makes sense for your group. For example:

- attend one another's worship services
- view a film together
- participate in a service or volunteer opportunity
- start up new ICQ for community building groups, encouraging one or two of your current members to serve together with representatives of the other group as the new ICQ bookgroups' facilitators

Consider if and how some of the questions from 1A, "Building ICQ through Introductions," could be useful for getting to know one another.

- Approach embassies, societies, universities, businesses, or NGOs to see if they are willing to support your ICQ for community building projects by sharing their expertise, resources, or connections.

What would be good ground rules or things to look for, think about, and analyze to make this experience both respectful and meaningful?

Idea 5: Storytables

Invite story tellers that represent experiences, perspectives, and cultural identities that you wish to learn more about. At a Storytable, the story tellers share food around a table and discuss together their experiences and thoughts centered around a chosen topic. At the same time invited listeners are seated around the room; they may also be eating but they are listening to learn. There is no question-and-answer period at the end, nor interrupting by the audience. It would be helpful to understand and outline the principles of storytables as found by googling "Storytables Fuller Seminary." The inclusion of facilitators experienced in ICQ or Intergroup Dialogue might be useful.

Idea 6: Conversation Cafés

Consider hosting a Conversation Café. At a Conversation Café event, small groups of people meet around a table and converse together. The Conversation Café approach to having constructive, learning conversations with different perspectives is described at their website. This site includes a clear outline of ground rules and process, as well as helpful handouts for facilitators, "wallet cards" with a summary of the rules of engagement for participants, tips for hosting a conversation café, a blog, and video training. It is important to clearly outline ground rules for the time together, including respectful, non-threatening engagement with others and their perspectives.

Whichever ideas you pursue as your next steps, keep in mind what we have learned about Interpersonal Cultural Intelligence so that we can be good hosts and good guests in these types of spaces as we build our community, relationships, and ICQ.

NEXT STEPS

What are your next steps?

- You as an individual: How will you continue your personal ICQ journey? How can you use your emerging ICQ skills to improve relationships in your family, at work, in your neighborhood, and in other communities you are part of?
- The ICQ project group: What happens with this project group now that chapter 5 is done? What are your best options? What are your goals?

"I CAN . . ." SELF-CHECK FOR CHAPTER 5

For each "I can" statement, indicate how much you agree with it by circling yes or no or by marking a spot along the yes-no line in the right column.

I can give a couple of examples of how rules of behavior differ across cultures.	Yes -------------------- No
I can give an example of how a social rule might be linked to a perspective inside a culture.	Yes -------------------- No
I can explain the differences between a tourist and a sojourner approach to engaging across cultural lines.	Yes -------------------- No
I can outline why hospitality and belonging are important for community building.	Yes -------------------- No
I can explain why building relationships across cultural lines can strengthen our communities.	Yes -------------------- No

Notes

Quotations in Learning Kit 5 are taken from Rick Steves, *Travel as a Political Act* (New York: Nation Books, 2009), 7; Carl Jung, *Modern Man in Search of a Soul* (England: Routledge, 1933), 121; Patty Lane, *A Beginner's Guide to Crossing Cultures* (Illinois: Intervarsity Press, 2002), 11; and David I. Smith and Pennylyn Dykstra-Pruim, *Christians and Cultural Difference* (Grand Rapids, MI: Calvin College Press, 2016), 61.

Activity 5G, The Global Kitchen Club: The website for this organization, accessed December 10, 2018 may be found at https://gust.com/companies/global_kitchen.

Activity 5G, Conversation Cafés: The website for conversation cafés, accessed August 19, 2019, may be found at http://www.conversationcafe.org/.

Acknowledgments

In all my cultures, we thank those who help us. The production of this book was supported by funding from the Kuyers Institute for Christian Teaching and Learning, the Calvin Center for Christian Scholarship, the Christian Reformed Church in North America—Office of Social Justice and Race Relations, and Calvin University. Thanks also to Susan M. Felch, Dale Williams, Michaela Osborne, Melinda Timmer, John Suk, and The Calvin Press for their editing and production work. Several friends and colleagues gave valuable feedback and support throughout the project and deserve recognition and chocolate, especially Marla Ehlers and the Peregrin writing group.

Of course, my family is the community that enables me to thrive in other communities. Thanks and hugs to Rand, Andrew, Anika, and Jason. Kids: one day brownie points will actually materialize into warm chocolate brownies. Finally, my deepest gratitude to all the family members, friends, colleagues, students, and acquaintances around the world who let me share pieces of their stories that intersect with mine. You have been a part of my ICQ journey, and now you can be part of that journey for others too.

CPSIA information can be obtained
at www.ICGtesting.com
Printed in the USA
LVHW010803110121
676188LV00002B/97